The Baseball Rating Handbook

The Baseball Rating Handbook

By Robert Allan Kalich

South Brunswick and New York: A. S. Barnes and Company
London: Thomas Yoseloff Ltd

© 1969 by A. S. Barnes and Co., Inc.
Library of Congress Catalogue Card Number: 76-76347

A. S. Barnes and Co., Inc.
Cranbury, New Jersey 08512

Thomas Yoseloff Ltd
108 New Bond Street
London W. 1, England

SBN: Paper: 498-07445-5
Cloth: 498-07438-2

Printed in the United States of America

to
LEROY "SATCHEL" PAIGE AND JOSH GIBSON
and the many other great Black Stars
who should have played
but unfortunately couldn't.

And to BRANCH RICKEY
who had the ability and courage and conviction
to make Baseball a true American pastime.

Acknowledgments

I would like to thank my Father who knew the difference between a good ball player and a bad one.
And I would like to thank Sid Cash and Bob B. B. Apfel who possessed the experience, knowledge and love of the game to assist in the very beginning.

Contents

Acknowledgments

PART 1

1. Introduction of the Six Categorical Rating System for Baseball Players and Pitchers ... 17
2. Summarizing the Six Categoricals for Pitchers ... 21
    First Categorical: Team Value ... 21
    Second Categorical: Power ... 22
    Third Categorical: Pitching Arsenal Value—Technical Proficiency ... 23
    Fourth Categorical: Control ... 24
    Fifth Categorical: Experience ... 25
    Sixth Categorical: Versatility and Execution ... 26
3. Summarizing the Six Offensive Categoricals ... 27
    First Categorical: Team Value ... 27
    Second Categorical: Power ... 28
    Third Categorical: Technical Proficiency ... 28
    Fourth Categorical: Speed ... 29

Fifth Categorical: Experience	30
Sixth Categorical: Versatility and Execution	30
4. Summarizing the Six Defensive Categoricals	32
First Categorical: Team Value	32
Second Categorical: Power	33
Third Categorical: Technical Proficiency	33
Fourth Categorical: Speed	34
Fifth Categorical: Experience	34
Sixth Categorical: Versatility and Execution	35
5. The Rating System's Methodology	37
6. The Six Categorical Rating Scales	40
7. Would You Believe	43
8. 1968 Was the Year of the Pitcher	45
9. 1968 Players of the Year	48
10. Player Retirements After the 1968 Season	54
11. 1969, The Year of Expansion	59
12. The Comprehensive and Chart Rating of 1969 Player Personnel	71
13. Major League Aspirants	134
14. Six Categorical Rating System's All Star Teams of Players Participating in 1969 Season	140
15. The Rating System's Selections of One Year Players: the All Star Team	143
16. The Rating System's Top Twenty Young Major Leaguers	145
17. Bob Kalich Selection of the World Championship Team for 1969	151

PART 2

1. Introducing the Six Categorical Rating System's All Time Major League Performers	157
2. Profiles on the All Time Greats	171

3. The Six Categorical Rating System's
   Selection of the All Time All Star Teams   189
4. The Legend Makers: The Greatest of the
   Long Ball Hitters   193
5. The Managers   200
6. Bob Kalich Selections of the Greatest Teams
   in Major League History   206
7. The Courage of a Ball Player   215

The Baseball Rating Handbook

Part 1

1

Introduction of the Six Categorical Rating System for Baseball Players and Pitchers

It took twenty years of debating and arguing and cussing to start this endeavor. Everyone had an opinion on who was the greatest and why. The "grandstand manager" was notorious, and every ball player, coach and manager I spoke to had his own ideas on what makes the complete ball player. I listened and learned from all—from "Casey" to the guy in the bleachers. From this listening, learning and studying of the facts I have systematically and objectively tried to take into account every possible factor that a ball player or pitcher can encounter during his major league career, and have then tried to give every factor due consideration in weighing the individual player's true abilities for a game, a season, a career, and of course his value to the team, and "the winning" of ball games.

Yes, the six categorical rating system has been created with many factors in mind, but of course the dominant influence is always: How did the player perform in the particular phase being examined? How much "Winning Value" did he inject into this particular category? With this ambitious program in mind many times it was only the memory of the past debates and arguments and questions that kept me going. How many times did I hear the refrain: "Who's better Koufax or Marichal"; "DiMaggio or Mays or Mantle"; and the thousands more that every child, every adult and every professional ball player mulls over because of his love of baseball. Well, because of these unanswered meditations I kept going, and now I hope that this system provides some of the answers in evaluating and judging the true worth of a ball player.

Every player who performed in the majors has been considered for the All Time Great Player List. Unfortunately I had to stop somewhere and could not list many of the men who were great contributors to Baseball. I ultimately decided to limit my selection to 25 top pitchers and the six top players at each of the eight other positions. Therefore the 27 all time great pitchers mentioned (numbers 25, 26 and 27 all tied for that last spot) received the highest rating scores, based on the six pitching categoricals, of all the pitchers who ever participated in the major leagues. The 52 all time great ball players at the other eight positions on the field also received the highest rating grades based on the six offensive and six defensive categoricals, which rate all of the players who performed at their respective positions down through major league history.

At this time I want to apologize if your favorite didn't

make it, but remember neither did "Lefty" O'Doul, (he came in seventh for left fielders) and he had a lifetime batting average of 349. At first base I listed eight because the players who finished sixth, seventh, and eighth all had the total rating grade of 123 and therefore deserved the honor of being included. At shortstop and third base there were ties for sixth place also and I included the seventh player at these positions.

In the section for the players of today I included every player who made a contribution during the 1968 season. Yes, every player was charted who had sufficient statistical criteria as a performer to be evaluated. And also remember all of the players were judged on their career performances, and not for any one week, "hot streak," particular achievement, month or season. Also keep in mind of primary consideration was "The Winning Value" the particular performer provided to his team for the categorical under scrutiny. Therefore the player's contribution to the winning of ball games, and the value of "Total Career Production" was given heavy consideration.

We have listed for the current players a special chapter on the rating of "Relief Pitchers" because of the influx of this specialist into the game today. There are no longer just a handful of these bullpen artists in the leagues; instead you will find many on each team, and all had to be evaluated.

In listing the present 1969 performers as well as the "All Time Greats" we have taken under consideration the following: That the player be evaluated and rated for the position he appeared at for the majority of his career. Therefore such men as Babe Ruth, Ernie Banks and Mickey Mantle are to be found under right field, shortstop and center field respectively, although each has played another position. In my opinion for the purpose of evaluating their enormous talents nothing could be fairer . . . Agree?

With the "All Time Greats" we have also taken one other liberty. The team they performed on during their most productive years is the one under which we have listed them. Therefore such as "The Babe" has remained a "Yankee" and not a "Boston Brave," the team with which he finished his fantastic career. Again I suggest nothing could be fairer.

I have taken into consideration in creating these categoricals over 800 factors, including such subtle tangibles as Koufax's ability to back up third, and Clemente's ability to back up the first basemen on the pitchers' and catchers' pick off throws.

I hope my system will be of as great interest and enjoyment to you as it was laborious to me in the preparation. I am sure that it will cause many arguments, and much provocation, and many new questions; but I am also sure it will give all of us a greater appreciation of the game, and of the many components and complex factors that go into making a "Truly Most Valuable Winning Ball Player."

2

Summarizing the Six Categoricals for Pitchers

The six categoricals for pitchers are rated on the following criteria, which take into consideration almost every possible factor and situation that can arise during a player's active campaigning. The scales are different for starting and relief pitchers, and the measurements are balanced according to the particular positions and the categorical's requirements. (See charts for measuring scale grades for current relief pitchers.)

FIRST CATEGORICAL: TEAM VALUE:

>Maximum grades:
>25 points for starting pitchers.
>15 points for relief pitchers.

A. Pitcher's ability to win consistently in season and in career.
B. Number of years pitcher wins more than 15 games, or the authority he shows in winning in any year during beginning of career.
C. Number of starts in season for pitcher, and won and lost record as compared with other pitchers in the league, and on his particular team.
D. Pitcher's ability to win the important games, the games that mean the pennant or the World Series.
E. Ability of pitcher to take his regular turn and pitch complete games.
F. The ability of pitcher to be selected by manager for "the important games" and his record in such games. Example would he be "the stopper"—the pitcher who consistently can stop a team's losing streaks.
G. The rating pitcher has on particular team he plays for. Is he the number ONE pitcher?
H. Overall stamina and endurance through career and for younger players for the seasons they appeared in.
I. The pitcher's ability to recuperate from a bad effort, from pain and bruises. To remain in starting rotation under such tensions, stress and pain. To suffer this type of duress, and to maintain a high standard of performance for the good of the team he represents.

SECOND CATEGORICAL: POWER:

Maximum Grades:
25 points for starting pitchers.
15 points for relief pitchers.

A. Earned Run Average of pitcher for season and career.
B. Wins and losses for season and career.
C. Winning percentage of pitcher for season and career.
D. Number of shutouts produced in season and career.

E. Number of complete games produced in season and career.
F. Number of games pitched in season and career in which pitcher went nine or more innings and gave up less than eight hits.
G. Number of innings pitched per season, and in career.
H. For relief pitchers: the number of games pitcher appeared in, received credit for "save" (protecting lead for team) and/or his particular record for career and season.
I. Number of strikeouts in season and career.
J. Number of bases on balls issued in season and career.

THIRD CATEGORICAL: PITCHING ARSENAL VALUE—TECHNICAL PROFICIENCY

Maximum Grades:
20 points for starting pitchers.
10 points for relief pitchers.

A. Pitcher's ability to maintain effectiveness because of the variety of pitches he has as well as his primary ability to get the "big outs" with his best pitch or pitches.
B. Pitching arsenal usually consists of some of the following pitches. We are judging the effectiveness of Player in using these pitches to win baseball games with his particular arsenal.
  1. Fast Ball: Does it move? Is it alive? What about velocity?
  2. Curve Ball: Is the break big, down, or flat?
  3. Change up (Slow pitch) used for change of speed, to keep batter off stride, usually thrown off fast ball motion. Is it kept low and controlled?
  4. Slider (Small curve): a pitch that "jumps" about six inches. Sharp pitch, when thrown correctly.
  5. Sinker: This pitch is a natural one, used like fast

ball, only it is always low. Good pitchers can make the batter hit ball on ground, so it's an effective double play pitch when thrown effectively.
  6. Screw ball: Moves away from hitter. Break is opposite of curve ball. Not many players have it. Extremely effective for left handed pitcher when perfected.
  7. Knuckle ball: Moves unpredictably. Wilhelm is its commissioner. The ball can move in any direction and when effective is more difficult to hit and/or catch than a butterfly.
  8. Other pitches: Fork ball, spit ball, etc., used by particular pitcher being graded.
C. The pitching value of the best pitches of player being evaluated in all game situations.
D. Is the pitcher's motion effective? Does it contribute to his pitching arsenal? Does the motion provide him with an "extra" edge by keeping the batter off stride?
E. Is the motion effective because it is physically easy, not a strain on the arm? Is the coordination of the player facilitated or strained?
F. Does the pitching motion and delivery enhance the over-all effectiveness of the weapons the pitcher must use?

FOURTH CATEGORICAL: CONTROL:

> Maximum Grades:
> 20 points for starting pitchers.
> 10 points for relief pitchers.

A. Of all pitches.
B. Control exhibited in given game situations; pressure situations and in particular sequences when pitcher must "throw strikes."
C. Ratio of bases on balls to strikeouts in season; for innings pitched, and for career.

D. Pitcher's ability to achieve double play when needed, or to stay away from throwing home run balls to the opposition when game is on the line. The pitcher's ability to "spot pitch" the ball where he wants under extreme pressure.
E. Ratio of base on balls to innings pitched for season or career.

FIFTH CATEGORICAL: EXPERIENCE:

Maximum Grades:
10 points for starting pitchers.
10 points for relief pitchers.

A. Cumulative judgment based on pitching statistics as well as all related "winning value" and game winning contributions.
B. Improvement of player through season and/or career, statistically and through fundamentals and intangibles.
C. Consistency and reliability of player through season and career.
D. Is the Pitcher's full potential being realized?
E. The number of years in league as starting pitcher or as relief pitcher. This is an important indicator in judging the experience factor. It takes into consideration the decisions and abilities of Managerial evaluation in considering the player's worth.
F. Pitcher's ability to use his craft on opposition, as well as in using advantages of park, and defensive alignments of teammates.
G. Over-all intelligence in pitching to game plan.
H. Did player participate in pennant fight, World Series, or all star games, in other words under all of the vital pressures of the professional. How was he performing in September during the utmost pressures?

SIXTH CATEGORICAL: VERSATILITY AND EXECUTION:

Maximum Grades:
10 points for starting pitchers.
10 points for relief pitchers.

A. Ability to cover position defensively.
B. Range in field.
C. Covering bases defensively.
D. Pickoff motion and effectiveness to all bases.
E. Offensive ability to sacrifice, and hit freely when at bat.
F. Ability to run on bases.
G. Ability to back up bases on defense. Is pitcher covering position, aggressively?

3

Summarizing the Six Offensive Categoricals

The six offensive categoricals are rated on the following criteria, which take into consideration almost every possible factor and situation that can come into play during a player's active career.

FIRST CATEGORICAL: TEAM VALUE:

Maximum Grade:
25 points.

A. Total bases produced in season and for career by player.
B. The on base percentage of performer for career and in season.

C. The slugging percentage of player for career and in season.
D. The number of bases on balls received by player in season and career.
E. The runs batted in per season and for career.
F. The number of game winning hits produced per season and for career. ("Is the player a clutch hitter?")
G. The consistency and sustained effort of player over season, and career.
H. Total tangible and intangible contributions to team in game, season and career.
I. Stamina and endurance of player through game, season and career.

SECOND CATEGORICAL: POWER:

Maximum Grade:
25 points.

A. Home runs produced per season and in career.
B. Base hits for player in season, and averaged during career.
C. Doubles and triples player produced in season and career.
D. Career and seasonal batting averages produced by player.
E. Ratio of strikeouts to bases on balls for player in season and career.
F. Ratio of time at bats to long hits, specifically home runs, for season and or career.

THIRD CATEGORICAL: TECHNICAL PROFICIENCY:

Maximum Grade:
25 points.

A. Plate coverage, conception of strike zone.
B. Absence of batting flaws, in body, swing, stride, movements, balance, stance. Each considered for player's production potential.
C. Quickness of player with bat, judged through proper wrist movement and power, considered for production potential and bat control abilities.
D. Speed by clock from plate to bases, or from base to base, and in all possible situations for production purposes.
E. Sliding abilities on bases and in run-scoring.
F. Offensive batting power to all fields, considered for purpose of potential.
G. Does player have enough power to reach "power alleys"?
H. For old-time players, criteria of statistical achievement is used as an indication of these abilities.
I. Aggressiveness of the player at the plate: Does he attack ball, or is he a defensive hitter?

FOURTH CATEGORICAL: SPEED:

Maximum Grade:
10 points.

A. Stolen bases by player in season and or career.
B. "Scratch hits" and "leg hits" produced by player.
C. "Bunt hits" produced by player.
D. Ability of player to advance on the bases.
E. Ability of player to take advantage of all offensive situations through his physical speed and mental alertness, which are companions in all game situations.

FIFTH CATEGORICAL: EXPERIENCE:

Maximum Grade:
10 points.

A. Improvement of player, realized through career, in all the other offensive categoricals.
B. Consistency and reliability of player during entire career.
C. Has the player's full potential been realized? Both mental and physical potentials are considered here.
D. Total number of years playing in the major leagues is an indication of player's value, ability and worth in the offensive categoricals.
E. Does player have experience in game and pennant pressures? Did he participate in pennant fights? September's ultimate games? World Series? All Star games? Did he perform well? Was he experienced in the whole gamut of professional baseball situations?

SIXTH CATEGORICALS: VERSATILITY AND EXECUTION:

Maximum Grade:
10 points.

A. Cumulative judgment based on offensive statistics, as well as "intangible team value" of player, in all game situations.
B. The hit and run ability of player.
C. Ratio of strikeouts by player to times at bat, as well as to base on balls.
D. The player's ability to sacrifice himself to advance the preceding base runner.
E. Ability of player to stay out of double play. How many does he hit into in a season? For career?
F. Ability of player to hit to all fields.

G. Can player be "pitched to"? Is he platooned? Does he have switch-hitting advantage?
H. Doth the player have the ability to protect base runners by his bat control over plate? Can he waste pitches, protect the plate, and force the opposing pitcher to make more than one good pitch?

4

Summarizing the Six Defensive Categoricals

The six defensive categoricals are rated on the following criteria, which take into consideration almost every possible factor and situation that can come into play during a player's active career.

FIRST CATEGORICAL: TEAM VALUE:

Maximum Grade:
20 points.

A. Player's ability to cover his particular position, by producing the "big play," the "game saver."
B. Player's "take charge ability" at his position. Does he play the defensive position aggressively?

C. The player's consistency and reliability over the season and entire career at the position.
D. Player's comparative fielding average as compared to all other performers in major league history at the particular position being rated.
E. Does the player contribute defensively to game saving? Does he provide assistance or is he a burden to his pitcher?

SECOND CATEGORICAL: POWER:

Maximum Grade:
10 points.

A. The number of assists player achieves in season and over entire career.
B. The number of putouts player achieves in season and over active career.
C. Errors (of commission) player made in season, and his average in career.
D. The player's proficiency in assisting in double plays for position.

THIRD CATEGORICAL: TECHNICAL PROFICIENCY

Maximum Grade:
10 points.

A. Size and strength needed for position.
B. Player's arm for position; his accuracy in throwing; his power in throwing.
C. Player's defensive range—to left, to right, inward, and backward.
D. Player's ability to get "jump" on ball which ultimately will allow greater productivity and effectiveness.

E. Player's "hands" for position; the value is indicated through performer's ability to make fielding plays quickly and surely. The player with "good hands" can handle without fumbling the most difficult of chances, such as bad hops, inbetween hops, unexpected turns, and flight of ball.
F. Player's ability to make recovery on same play after miscue.
G. Player's defensive strength and flaws as indicated through physical body movements and stance on defense.

FOURTH CATEGORICAL: SPEED:

Maximum Grade:
10 points.

A. Player's ability to pivot for position. This ability allows player to stay out of the way of the offensive runner, as well as to make the proper execution without losing balance or effectiveness.
B. Player's ability to field bunts by charging, quickness, and sureness.
C. Player's range in covering his own particular position.
D. Player's ability to use speed in assisting teammates, by backing up plays, covering more territory than is expected, and assisting in general defense for team.
E. Player's ability to use speed to release ball on throws, and still maintain high standard of accuracy and power.

FIFTH CATEGORICAL: EXPERIENCE:

Maximum Grade:
10 points.

A. Improvement of player, throughout career, at this particular position.
B. Consistency and reliability of player through career.
C. Has the player's full defensive potential been realized?
D. Total number of years in major leagues as starting player—an indication of player's true value, ability and worth defensively.
E. Does player make the correct play? Is there a lack of errors of *omission?*
F. Does player know the strengths and weaknesses of the opposition. Does he use his experience to play the proper position according to batter, pitcher, and game situations?
G. Does player have an awareness of the different parks, walls, and situations that can come up under all ground rules? Does he execute this awareness in game situations?
H. Did player perform in the pressure of pennant fights, World Series, and all star games. Did he perform well? All experiences must be considered.

SIXTH CATEGORICAL: VERSATILITY AND EXECUTION:

Maximum Grade:
10 points.

A. Does player throw to right base? Does opposition run on player?
B. Does player cover position totally, aggressively? Can he, for example, back up plays correctly?
C. Does player present a good target at his position?
D. Does player have the ability to play more than one position?
E. Does player have the ability to execute properly in all game situations? Such as

1. hitting cut off man
2. blocking and tagging of base runners.

5

The Rating System's Methodology

STARTING PITCHERS:

The six categoricals for starting pitchers have a maximum achievement score of 110 points.

Each categorical is rated independently and given a maximum commensurate with its particular value to the total winning action.

The first categorical, "team value," has a total grade of 25 points.

The second categorical, "power," has maximum grade of 25 points.

The third categorical, "pitching arsenal"—"technical proficiency" has a maximum grade of 20 points.

The fourth categorical, "control," has maximum grade of 20 points.

The fifth categorical, "Experience," has maximum grade of 10 points.

The sixth categorical, "versalitity and execution," has maximum grade of 10 points.

RELIEF PITCHERS:

The six categoricals for Relief Pitchers have a maximum achievement score of 70 points.

Each categorical is rated independently and given a maximum commensurate with its particular value to the total winning of the game, and for the perspective on winning for the season and for the particular team the player represents.

The first categorical, "team value," has maximum grade of 15 points.

The second categorical, "power," has maximum grade of 15 points.

The third categorical, "pitching arsenal and technical proficiency," has maximum value for grade of 10 points.

The fourth categorical, "control," has maximum value grade of 10 points.

The fifth categorical, "experience," has maximum value grade of 10 points.

The sixth categorical, "versatility and execution," has maximum grade value of 10 points.

OFFENSIVE CATEGORICALS:

The six categoricals for Offensive achievements have a maximum total of 105 points.

Each categorical is rated independently and given a maximum grade commensurate with its particular value to the total winning performance of the player and for the team.

The first categorical, team value, has a maximum grade of 25 points.

The second categorical, "power," has a maximum grade of 25 points.

The third categorical, "technical proficiency," has a maximum grade of 25 points.

The fourth categorical, "speed," has maximum grade of 10 points.

The fifth categorical, "experience," has maximum grade of 10 points.

The sixth categorical, "versatility and execution," has a maximum grade of 10 points.

DEFENSIVE CATEGORICALS:

The six categoricals for defensive achievements have a maximum total grade of 70.

Each categorical is rated independently and given a maximum grade commensurate with its particular value to the total winning performance of the player and for the team.

The first categorical, "team value," has a maximum grade of 20 points.

The second categorical, "power," has a maximum grade of 10 points.

The third categorical, "technical proficiency," has maximum grade of 10 points.

The fourth categorical, "speed," has maximum grade of 10 points.

The fifth categorical, "experience," has maximum grade of 10 points.

The sixth categorical, "versatility and execution," has maximum grade of 10 points.

6

The Six Categorical Rating Scales

THE 25 POINT SCALE:
22–25 points: For perfect achievements.
19–21 points: Player performs on par with top stars of his generation.
16–18 points: Player performs on par with stars in game today.
12–15 points: A real solid performer. Star quality.
 9–11 points: Average abilities for starting ball player.
 5– 8 points: Marginal player, sometimes bench warmer, and or below major league standard. Weaknesses and/or inexperience are usually flagrant in this categorical grade.
 0– 4 points: Minor league abilities, or inexperience and lack of sufficient criteria to give higher rating.

THE 20 POINT SCALE:
19–20 points: For perfect achievement.
16–18 points: Player performs on par with top stars of his generation.
12–15 points: Player performs on par with top stars of contemporary vintage.
8–11 points: Average abilities.
5– 7 points: Marginal player, weakness in particular categorical.
0– 4 points: Weaknesses are flagrant and are on minor league level. Inexperienced player also rated here because of insufficient criteria to give higher rating.

THE 15 POINT SCALE
15 points: For perfect achievement.
12–14 points: Player performs on par with top stars of last FIFTEEN YEARS.
7–11 points: Average to solid abilities.
4– 6 points: Marginal player, or usually player has some inexperience. Otherwise journeyman performer.
0– 3 points: Flagrant weaknesses on par with minor league standards, or inexperience of particular player causes lack of sufficient criteria to give higher rating.

THE 10 POINT RATING SCALE:
10 points: For perfect achievement.
9 points: For player who performs on level with top stars of game.
8 points: Real good defensive player, or solid in this categorical.
4–7 points: Average to minor weaknesses.
1–3 points: Weakness in particular categorical grade.

Usually this player is on par with utility player, or marginal one, who has journeymen's history as professional ball player. Otherwise it is a player who has minor league abilities in a particular skill, or is inexperienced and there is not sufficient criteria to give higher rating.

7

Would You Believe

Remember 1961? It was the year Roger Maris hit 61 home runs. It was only a short while ago, and of course you remember some of the pitchers he hit home runs off. Let's see now, there's Gary Bell then with Cleveland and now throwing for Seattle. Rog hit two off Gary. Then there was Bill Monbouquette, he was a fireballer then for Boston, now he is trying to make an expansion team for 1969. Some of them can use his craft and his guile. Jim Perry with the Minnesota Twins in 1961 was also belted for one by Maris, and then that great right hander Camillio Pasqual was reached for another. Juan Pizarro the classy left hander was also reached for one on August 15, 1961, it was Roger's 46th and was hit into the bullpen in Yankee Stadium, the one in right center.

Let me think . . . "Mud Cat" Grant, I think he is retiring now (he wants to sing), was hit for another, number 56 in the 141st game of the year. The date was September 9. The 59th was hit off Milt Pappas then with Baltimore on September 20. After that it was bedlam . . . Remember? The pressure became enormous, and on the night of September 26 Roger hit number 60 in Baltimore. The pitcher the ex-Met Jack Fisher still doing pretty good for the White Sox. He might be available for 1969 . . . The 61st was hit on October 1, 1961, in the Yankees 163rd game of the year off the now retired Tracy Stallard. He was on the Red Sox then. It was gone the minute Roger made contact and it floated into the lower grandstand in right field of Yankee stadium over the 344 foot mark. A place where Ruth himself had reached on many an occasion. The fans stood up and applauded, and Mantle shook his hand from the on deck circle.

Roger Maris is retiring now; he won't play in 1969. He never was the same after that 1961 season, "but he was something else in '61." The point is—"would you believe" that Jim Perry, Gary Bell, Bill Monbouquette, Juan Pizarro, Mudcat Grant, Milt Pappas, and Jack Fisher are the only seven active of the 50 reached for homers by Roger in '61; "Would you believe" I'll never forget '61—or Roger.

8

1968 Was the Year of the Pitcher

It certainly was, and why shouldn't it have been? Bob Gibson, Dennis McLain, Don Drysdale, Luis Tiant, Jerry Koosman, and some of the others have pretty good arms. Some of the records were outstanding. Marichal kept winning and winning, McLain the same. Gibson won 15 in a row, and between him and Drysdale, and for a while Tiant, runs seemed to be anonymous. In fact Gibson between May 3 and August 23 established not only the 15-game winning streak but pitched more shutouts, shutout innings, and low hit games than any pitcher had ever done before over any similar span of games. He finally lost on August 24, giving up three earned runs in a game against Pittsburgh. He pitched badly, though—a six hitter and he only struck out 15 Pirates. Yes it was the year of the pitcher, and the hypothesizing on why has filled up many a sports column. It's simple though if you look closely. Pitchers were able to pitch, and hitters stopped hitting. There were many quality pitchers in '68, more than in many a year, and in the American League you could count the quality hitters on one hand—in the National on two. Many of the pitchers achieved their peak seasons.

Technically many of the young men have begun to throw curves, changes and sliders with consistency—and not over the plate either, but on a corner and either high or low depending on the hitter's weakness. Fastballs down the middle are forgotten, on 2 and 0, and 3 and 1 and even 3 and 0 you get nothing to hit at but "pitcher's pitches" and they're only good for the pitcher nowadays. This obviously has caused trouble for the troubled sorry hitter. Besides, said Joel Horlen of the White Sox pitching staff, "the hitters are dumber now than ever before." He's absolutely right and until they start listening to Harry Walker and the other batting specialists they will continue to have considerable dates with that .200 batting average, and .260 will seem like a good year to the rationalizing players. Of course these are the players that will refuse to adjust—go with the pitch, and will continue to do almost everything wrong. But don't let them fool you—the good ones will continue to hit.

Matty Alou and Pete Rose and Tony Oliva and Carl Yastrzemski and all the others who can really hit and still have youth and time will do the hitting. They won't be hitting .250 or .260, it's for those "dumb hitters," not for the real good ones. The good ones don't try to pull everything, and they go with the pitch. They also swing at strikes, only strikes, and their determination and concentration is perfect.

Yes it continues to be a question of technique, determination and ability. But it did seem that the pitchers had passed most of the batters in all of these categories. I predict that the cycle will change immediately and this, the year of expansion, will see many less 1–0 games and many, many less 18-inning marathons.

Of course the Gibsons and Marichals will continue winning and the others with similar ability will still be pitching zeros. And of course hitters like Cincinnati has in Rose and Helms and Johnson and May and Bench and Perez will continue hitting. Yes it's good pitching and some good hitting, and the good ones, whether pitchers or hitters, will rise to the occasion.

9

1968 Players of the Year

Only the pitchers were truly outstanding in 1968. The pitchers who dominated the season were Bob Gibson of the St. Louis Cardinals and Dennis McLain of the Detroit Tigers. Their sustained performances throughout the season were of fantastic proportions. Their value was evident on almost every occasion. It is because of their abilities, performances and achievements that their respective teams were the champions. Without hesitation we have selected them as the "1968 PLAYERS OF THE YEAR." Some of their vital statistics follow:

DENNIS (DENNY) McLAIN: DETROIT TIGERS
   31 wins–6 losses. Best winning percentage in baseball.

   Pitched 336 innings—most since Bobby Feller's 313 in 1946—for the American league.

28 complete game victories.

Winner of the "Cy Young" award and the Most Valuable Player Award in the American league. First American Leaguer to achieve this distinction.

BOB (HOOT) GIBSON: ST. LOUIS CARDINALS
1968 "Cy Young" Award winner in National league.

28 complete games in 34 starts.

Worked 305 total innings.

Allowed only 198 hits for entire season's work.

Walked 62 and led league in strikeouts with 268 K's.

Pitched 13 complete-game shutouts
Won 15 straight games during '68 season.

Was knocked out of box only once in all the games he started.

Set new Major League record of 1.12 Earned run Average—lowest in the history of the Majors.

Former marks were held by Grover Cleveland Alexander in National League (1.22 in 1915) and Walter Johnson in American League (1.14 in 1913).

With those measurements Denny and Hoot could win any beauty contest.

1968 PLAYERS OF THE YEAR:
The year provided individual achievements and some fantastic records. Consider the following as a sample . . .
Don Drysdale of the Los Angeles Dodgers, set an all time shutout inning string of 56⅔ innings. (In the official record book it will be listed as 56 innings.)
Maurey Wills, now in the twilight of his career, still stole 52 bases, second only to Lou Brock of the Cardinals and "Campy" Campanaris of the Athletics; both

with league leading totals of 62 stolen bases. Wills during the September stretch went over the "500" career stolen base mark, a fantastic achievement as well as a record. The only previous players in the history of the game to do this were Ty Cobb, Honus Wagner, Eddie Collins and Max Carey. That makes Wills only the fifth modern player to reach the mark.

Wilbur Wood the knuckle balling relief pitcher of the Chicago White Sox appeared in more games than any other pitcher in major league history for any one season. He broke Ted Abernathy's former record of 85 performances with a few to spare.

Micky Mantle went into third place in the all time Home Run totals in major league history with 536 for his great career, replacing Jimmy Foxx. The "535th" came on September 19, 1968 off Denny McLain who was winning his 31st game of the year that night. It gave Denny the most wins by a major league pitcher since 1934 when Bob ("Lefty") Grove won his 31. Dennis McLain also broke his own Detroit Tiger club record for strikeouts in a single season with 279; the previous record belonged to Hal Newhouser, the lefthanded Prince who had 276 for the Detroit club almost 25 years ago.

Other great records and accomplishments of 1968 were set by Bob Gibson, who pitched 13 shutouts, and set a new Major League Earned Run Average record with his amazing and brilliant and inconceivable 1.12. He also led the league in strikeouts with 268 and had one of the greatest years in the history of the game—that is, for any pitcher who ever threw a ball on the "corner." The former E.R.A. king was Walter Johnson, who in 1913 had an E.R.A. of 1.14. "The Big Train" was really some kind of pitcher.

Let's not forget the brilliant year of Luis Tiant with his 21 wins and league leading E.R.A. of 1.60, and his 263 strikeouts. His Earned Run Average also set a

Cleveland Indian club record, and that is significant as some of the past Indian hurlers were Bobby Feller, Bob Lemon, Early Wynn, Mike Garcia, Mel Harder and Herb Score. Yes Luis had some kind of year.

What about his teammate "Sad" Sam McDowell the powerful lefthander. He had another of those years in which the experts and wise guys were saying "he just can't put it all together," yet Sam won 15 games, and led the major leagues in strikeouts with 283 and his E.R.A. of 1.81 was second best in the American League to teammate Tiant; only Bob Gibson did better in the National.

Of course Sam will have trouble explaining to everyone why he had such a "sad, sad" year. Sometimes when you're great like "Sad Sam" is, you just have to win 20.

What about the all time great right hander Juan Marichal, of the San Francisco Giants, with his 26 wins, and 325 "work horse" innings pitched. How much better can a guy do? And what about the classy rookies Jerry Koosman with his 19 wins, best by any left hander in the league and his 8 shutouts, which tied a national league record for rookie pitchers. The other great young rookie was Stan Bahnsen of the Yankees with his hard-earned 17 wins.

There were others on the mound who had great years. To name just some—Steve Blass of Pittsburgh, Dave McNally of Baltimore, Mel Stottlemyre of the Yankees and Ferguson Jenkins the strong man of the Chicago Cubs.

Then there was Ray Culp of Boston and Tom Seaver of the Mets, each of whom won 16. Congratulations to all of them for their great achievements and individual records for 1968.

THE BATTING CHAMPS:

Hitting in 1968 was at a premium but here are some of the fellows who proved it could be done.

Pete Rose of the Cincinnati Reds who finished the year with a major league batting title of .335. He had to go "five for five" on the next to last day of the season, as his nearest competitor, Matty Alou was going "four for four." But Matty finished with a .332 batting average, and Pete had the title. Another Alou tied Rose for the most base hits for the season; it was Matty's brother Felipe of Atlanta, who finished with 210 base hits. They were the only players in both leagues to get more than that magic 200.

In the American League .300 was something else. Only Carl Yastrzemski was able to get that high, with a league leading .300.5 just about as close as you can get. It was the second title in a row for the Boston batting champ. The .300 batting average was also a record, as it was the lowest ever achieved by a batting title winner in major league history.

Runs Batted In were just as hard to get as hitting .300, with only Ken Harrelson of the Red Sox (with his major league leading 109), Frank Howard of Washington (106), and Willie McCovey of San Francisco, the National League leader (105), going over the 100 mark.

In Home Runs, again it was gigantic Frank Howard leading everyone with 44. And again Willie McCovey led the National league with 36 round trippers. The only other players to go over the 30 mark were Willie Horton, Detroit Tigers (36), Ken Harrelson, Boston Redsox (35), slugging Richie Allen, Philadelphia Phils (33), Ernie Banks, Chicago Cubs (32), and Billie Williams, Chicago Cubs, (30). How about that amazing old man Mr. Banks, though; he really had a season.

One of the best years was had by a player who didn't have the great statistics. It was Bill Freehan the hard hitting catcher of the Detroit Tigers. He did everything on offense and defense that was wanted, and he also hit 25 home runs and knocked in 84 game winning runs. Many times Bill was that clutch hitter supreme that a pennant team needs to survive. In my book his value was second only to Denny MeLain's for the Detroit Championship. Remember it was Bill who led the team in games played; and when you consider he played majority of these games at the catcher's position you get an idea of how hard he worked. To further emphasize his ability and courage, remember he also set a new American League record of getting hit by pitches—24 times in all (the old record was 23 by that old war horse, Minnie Minoso).

These were the players who had the best seasons, and though hitting was hard to find, it was there if you were willing to look hard enough; of course, it was easier if you happened to look only at the above named players.

10

Player Retirements After the 1968 Season

Five of the best players of the past generation announced their retirements from active competition at the close of the 1968 season. They are:

ELSTON HOWARD: 1955–1968 CATCHER.	N. Y. Yankees Boston Red Sox	1955–1967 1967–1968
BILL WHITE: 1956–1968 FIRST BASE.	N. Y. Giants S. F. Giants St. Louis Cardinals Phila. Phils.	1956–1957 1958 1959–1965 1966–1968
EDDIE MATHEWS: 1952–1968 THIRD BASE.	Boston Braves Milwaukee Braves Atlanta Braves	1952 1953–1965 1966

	Houston Astros.	1967
	Detroit Tigers	1967–1968
ROGER MARIS:	Cleveland Indians	1957–1958
1957–1968	K. C. Athletics	1958–1959
RIGHT FIELD.	N. Y. Yankees	1960–1966
	St. Louis Cardinals	1967–1968
LARRY JACKSON:	St. Louis Cardinals	1955–1962
1955–1968	Chicago Cubs	1963–1966
PITCHER.	Phila. Phils.	1966–1968

All five of these players performed with exceptional ability and their performances and records will remain a significant chapter in major league baseball history.

LARRY JACKSON:

For 15 years he was a Major League pitcher. His talent was more than his ability to throw hard and long. Larry Jackson was a "pitcher" and that means he could "hit corners," set up hitters, keep the ball down, and win. He was crafty and smart, clever and tough. Larry Jackson won 194 major league games and many of them were for second division ball clubs. He announced his retirement plans a day after he was selected by the Montreal Expos. Maybe manager Gene Mauch can talk Larry into another year; if he does Larry will still be a regular and still win his share. He looked good in 1968, and could help the Expos in their maiden season. If Larry goes through with his retirement plans the N. Y. Mets will be the happiest. He beat them most of all.

ELSTON HOWARD:

This great catcher for over a decade performed for the Yankees. A major contributor to the great teams of the late '50's and early '60's he was awarded the Most Valuable Player award in 1963. Ellie was a great clutch performer and excelled in many World Series games. He was the kind of player championship teams are made of. This year he will be returning to the Yankees, but now, at the age of forty, he will be returning as a coach. Good Luck Elston; you were one of the best.

EDDIE MATHEWS:
He had his great years with the Braves organization. He played with them on their travels through Boston, Milwaukee and Atlanta, always hitting home runs and slugging with the best in the game. He has hit more home runs than any third baseman in the game's history, finishing with a total of (512). Overall his bat makes him a prime candidate for the hall of fame. He always will be regarded as one of the great modern sluggers in the game's history. For where he compares with the all time greats see Part II of the annual, and study his chart rating evaluations.

ROGER MARIS:
He had his great years with the Yankees, and was awarded the Most Valuable Player prize in both 1960 and 1961. It was 1961 when he hit the famous "61." Rog will be in the record book and remembered as long as Home Runs are being hit.

BILL WHITE
The winner of the golden glove award for his defense at first base from 1960 through 1966, Bill was one of the most accomplished players in the game's history. Bill White could do it all. The players called him "a professional" the entire establishment knew he had "class." It is very likely that the first Negro manager will be from among the following names—Wills, Howard, Rob-

inson, Mays and White. They all have the ability, but Bill White might just have more.

The individual ratings of these five great veteran stars are on the charts that follow. Two other veterans have been considering retirement but have remained undecided at this time: Jim Bunnng and Kenny Boyer. We hope they will return to the wars along with Mickey Mantle, who has privately mentioned he expects to play through 1969. Of course, we want them to return; of course, we wish them all the best of luck in 1969. Because we have confidence that Boyer and Bunning will return for 1969 we have listed them with the other active players and their six categorical ratings can be found there. By the way don't be surprised if you find Ken Boyer along with Eddie Mathews on the all time great third base lists of Part II—you just might. Another retiring veteran is Dick Howser, the solid utility infielder. Along with Elston Howard he has taken a position with the Yankees as a coach.

POSITION RATED: ALL TIME GREATS RETIRED AFTER 1968 SEASON

	OFFENSIVE CATEGORICALS							DEFENSIVE CATEGORICALS							
	1-TEAM VALUE	2-POWER	3-TECHNICAL PROFICIENCY	4-SPEED	5-EXPERIENCE	6-VERSATILITY AND EXECUTION	THE OFFENSIVE TOTALS	1-TEAM VALUE	2-POWER	3-TECHNICAL PROFICIENCY	4-SPEED	5-EXPERIENCE	6-VERSATILITY AND EXECUTION	THE DEFENSIVE TOTALS	TOTAL POINTS OF PLAYER
Rating Scale in points:	25	25	25	10	10	10	105 Max	20	10	10	10	10	10	70	175 Max (ideal)
Elston Howard: Catcher 1955-1968 N.Y. Yankees Boston Red Sox	12	10	12	2	10	5	51	14	8	8	6	10	8	54	105
Roger Maris: Right Field 1957-1968 Cleveland, K.C. Athletics N.Y. Yankees & St. L. Cardinals	13	18	11	5	10	4	61	16	8	8	8	10	8	58	119
Bill White: First Base 1956-1968 N.Y. Giants, St. L. Cardinals, & Phila. Phils	14	12	13	5	10	7	61	14	8	8	7	10	8	55	116
Eddie Mathews: Third Base * 1952-1968 Boston Braves, Milw. Braves, Detroit Tigers, Atlanta Braves & Houston Astros	17	19	14	7	10	6	73	10	7	7	7	9	6	46	119

*Eddie Mathews' rating is sufficient to classify him as one of the all time third basemen in the game's history. See Part II: Third basemen.

STARTING PITCHERS

RETIREMENTS AFTER 1968 SEASON

THE SIX PITCHING CATEGORICALS

	1-TEAM VALUE	2-POWER	3-PITCHING ARSENAL VALUE TECHNICAL PROFICIENCY	4-CONTROL	5-EXPERIENCE	6-VERSATILITY AND EXECUTION	TOTAL POINTS
Rating Scale in points:	25	25	20	20	10	10	110 Max (ideal)
LARRY JACKSON 1955-1968 St. Louis Cardinals 1955-1962 Chicago Cubs 1963-1966 Phila. Phils 1966-1968	13	13	12	16	10	6	70

11

1969, The Year of Expansion

The national pastime has taken another giant step forward. Each league has again expanded, taking two neophytes to its bosom. In the National League new teams will be the Montreal Expos and the San Diego Padres; and in the American League, the Kansas City Royals and the Seattle Pilots will play their first season. Each of these four franchises paid the asking price of $10.5 million to select 30 players, six from each of the senior members. The cost of each player came to a nice comfortable sum of $333,000. I can't help wondering how many of these players will pay the bill—can you?

If past expansion trends are any indication, turnover through trades, ineptitude, retirements, and injuries will be tremendous; and before long the entire roster of each team with very few exceptions will be overhauled. But right now, these 30 players are a beginning; and at that, it seems like a good one for all of the freshman franchises. Of course, with the new divisional setup, you can't finish lower than number six, and that makes for immediate improvement, doesn't it? One thing is for sure, we can't expect miracles, and the nucleus from the expansion drafts will remain through 1969. Because of this our yearlings must have an abundance of courage, guts, hustle and fortitude and, of course, some professional ball players in 1969.

Let us at this time introduce some of the veterans and youngsters who might provide the glue, tape, improvisation and ability to field a reasonable professional entry in 1969. This is how it might begin.

NATIONAL LEAGUE:

Montreal Expos Wth Gene Mauch at the Helm:

Manager Mauch drafted classy Larry Jackson whom he managed at Philadelphia. Larry immediately announced his retirement, which makes one wonder about Mauch's prior knowledge of the veteran's attitudes, doesn't it. In all Gene selected what is probably the strongest of the four expansion teams. For pitching he has another veteran in Jim "Mudcat" Grant, who might be a real winner if he decides on remaining. You see, The Mudcat also announced that he was considering retirement. Mauch might be in for a long season, but he still has a very good portsider with an excellent arm in Larry Jaster, and some of the potential strength of the pitching staff must come from such fuzzy cheeked boys as Bob Reynolds and Jerry Robertson. For Relief John Billingham is coming off an exceptional rookie season, and could be first rate; and the ex-Met Don Shaw can keep the ball low and do the job against left handed batters. All in all, it might work out for Mr. Mauch: he has the time, the patience, the talent and the verve to make things happen, and they will happen in that great city of Montreal.

The infield can have an exceptionally talented lot for an expansion team with John Bateman catching, Clendenon at first, if Donn plays (he too announced plans of retiring). If he plays he could still be a star; he is finally finished with his many problems with the Pirates, and this could be an important factor for such a gifted athlete. Second base will be unpredictable, with Jimmy Williams at this time leading the candidates; at Shortstop will be Gary Sutherland who might just be a good one, while at third base another veteran who is threatening retirement can mean a great deal. If he doesn't retire Mauch will be as happy as Lolich was in October, for Maury Wills provides class. He can give a team everything, including a winning attitude. Yes Mr. Wills, if he plays, will give Montreal a first-rate expansion team. If he is available he could even assist indirectly. He has a large market value and a trade might be substantial.

In the outfield we have real talent with Jesus Alou, Manny Mota and Mack Jones providing a legitimate major league trio of fly-chasers. They also provide market value and trading might be on Mauch's mind. With this analysis you might think Montreal has a chance to finish out of the cellar, and you know what, you might be right. Now who will they beat—that is the question.

Montreal Expos Draft Choices in Order of Selection:

1. Manny Mota, Center fielder from Pittsburgh. (Also plays infield.)
2. Mack Jones, Center fielder from Cincinnati.
3. John Bateman, Catcher from Houston.
4. Gary Sutherland, Shortstop from Philadelphia.
5. John Billingham, Relief Pitcher from Los Angeles.

6. Donn Clendenon, First baseman, from Pittsburgh.
7. Jesus Alou, Outfielder from San Francisco.
8. Mike Wegner, Pitcher from Philadelphia. No major league experience through 1968 season.
9. Skip Guinn, Pitcher from Atlanta (came up at end of 1968 season for very brief experience).
10. Bill Stoneman, Pitcher from Chicago Cubs.
11. Maury Wills, Infielder from Pittsburgh (s.s. and 3b).
12. Larry Jackson, Pitcher from Philadelphia.
13. Bob Reynolds, Pitcher from San Francisco. No experience through 1968 season as major leaguer.
14. Ted McGinn, Pitcher, from Atlanta.
15. Jose Herrera, Third base and outfield, from Houston.
16. Jim Williams, Shortstop from Cincinnati, appeared briefly for Reds beginning with 1966 season. Very limited experience as major leaguer.
17. Angel Hermoso, Infielder from Atlanta. No major league experence through 1968 season.
18. Jim "Mudcat" Grant, Pitcher from Los Angeles.
19. Jerry Roberston, Pitcher from Cardinals. No major league experience through 1968 season.
20. Don Shaw, Relief Pitcher from N. Y. Mets.
21. Ty Cline, Outfielder from San Francisco.
22. Gary Jestadt, Short stop from Chicago Cubs. No previous major league experience through 1968 season.
23. Carl Morton, Pitcher from Atlanta Braves. No previous major league experience through 1968 season.
24. Larry Jaster, Pitcher from St. Louis.
25. Ernest McAnally, Pitcher from N.Y. Mets. No major league experience through 1968 season.
26. Jim Fairey, Outfielder from Los Angeles.
27. Jose Laboy, Second base from St. Louis. No major league experience through 1968 season.
28. John Boccabella, Catcher-first Baseman from Chicago Cubs.
29. Ron Brand, Catcher from Houston.

30. John Glass, Pitcher from N.Y. Mets. No major league experience through 1968 season.

San Diego Padres with Preston Gomez Managing:

Good pitching is important. Gomez made sure he took two of the better National League hurlers in Dick Selma who might become a star (or be traded for one), and Dave Giusti who might be used for trade bait, but if he isn't he could win in double figures. Then he took Al McBean and Dick Kelley, who have strong arms. The surprise might be in the still young left hander Billy McCool who has all the tools to be a winning McCool. He could become a starting pitcher for the Padres. He definitely could become a winning pitcher if he can put it all together. Gomez also drafted some great young prospects, and the word "great" isn't used loosely. Dave Roberts was the International League's Most Valuable Player, with an 18-6 record in 1968. Now if he is ready to make the jump won't Pittsburgh be crying? Other youngsters with promise are Al Santorini, Clay Kirby, and Frank Reberger, and there might be room for a couple of free agents, namely Jim Bouton and Johnny Podres; wouldn't that be fun.

In the infield there will be a few gaps and trades will be made before you read this, but right now Gomez's catchers are two inexperienced youngsters, Fred Kendell and Ron Slocum. They are good prospects, but neither has been in a major league game. Kendell has the better credentials if San Diego can't find someone with more experience.

Right now Nate Colbert is the choice for first base with Roberto Pena and Zoilo Versailles providing adequate ability around both sides of the keystone sack. Yes, Versailles is more than adequate, if he wants to be; that is the question. Third will be the province of Jose Arcia who might be something special. But the outfield is where the Padres will have their punch, with Al Ferrara, Tony Gonzalez and Ollie Brown the top prospects. Ollie and Tony can be great for the San Diego entry, and if help is needed there are more good and young outfielders around including Larry Stahl, and a nineteen year old young man who might be shipped to the minors to learn his trade. But who knows—Jerry Morales might be in San Diego.

In all, the Padres are a fair club with real talent and real weaknesses and real problems.

San Diego Draft Choices in Order of Selection:

1. Ollie Brown, Outfielder from San Francisco.
2. Dave Giusti, Pitcher from St. Louis.
3. Dick Selma, Pitcher from N.Y. Mets.
4. Al Santorini, Pitcher from Atlanta.
5. Jose Arcia, Infielder from Chicago Cubs.
6. Clay Kirby, Pitcher from St. Louis chain. No major league experience through 1968.
7. Fred Kendell, Catcher from Cincinnati, no major league experience through 1968.
8. Jerry Morales, Centerfielder from N.Y. Mets, no major league experience through 1968.
9. Zoilo Versailles, Shortstop from Los Angeles.
10. Nate Colbert, First baseman from Houston.
11. Frank Reberger, Pitcher from Chicago Cubs, no major league experience through 1968.
12. Frank Davanon, Infielder from St. Louis, no major league experience through 1968.
13. Larry Stahl, Outfielder from N.Y. Mets.
14. Dick Kelley, Pitcher from Atlanta.
15. Al Ferrara, Left fielder from Los Angeles, injured and inactive during majority of 1968.
16. Mike Corkins, Pitcher from San Francisco, no major league experience through 1968.
17. Tom Dukes, Pitcher from Houston.

18. Richard James, Pitcher from Chicago Cubs, no major league experience through 1968.
19. Tony Gonzalez, Centerfielder from Philadelphia.
20. Dave Roberts, Pitcher from Pittsburgh, no major league experience through 1968 season.
21. Ivan Murrell, Outfielder from Houston.
22. James Williams, Outfielder from Los Angeles, no major league experience through 1968.
23. Billy McCool, Pitcher from Cincinnati.
24. Roberto Pena, Infielder from Philadelphia.
25. Al McBean, Pitcher from Pittsburgh.
26. Rafael Robles, Shortstop from San Francisco, no major league experience through 1968 season.
27. Fred Katawczik, Pitcher from Cincinnati no major league experience through 1968 season.
28. Ron Slocum, Catcher from Pittsburgh, no major league experience through 1968 season.
29. Steve Arlin, Pitcher from Philadelphia, no major league experience through 1968 season.
30. Clarence Gaston, Outfielder from Atlanta.

AMERICAN LEAGUE

Kansas City Royals with Joe ("Flash") Gordon as Skipper

Gordon took some chances with his picks; he took many inexperienced rookies, real raw ones. How they will do remains to be seen. Right now Gordon's pitching hopes are not predictable because his best prospects have histories of sore wings, but if they don't, they are young and they can win—Dave Morehead and Wally Bunker especially. Roger Nelson was Joe's first selection, and he won only four games for Baltimore in '68. It remains to be seen how he does for K.C.—maybe Joe knows something. . . . Some of the good young pitchers with real arms are Jon Wardon, Jim Rooker, and Steve Jones, and I didn't forget Richie Drago, he also might have a future. The question is how quickly they can be rushed. It's one hell of a queston Mr. Gordon. In the bullpen he can have two veterans who really know the game coaching as well as pitching. They are Moe Drabowsky and the veteran's veteran Hoyt Wilhelm; if Hoyt remains on the roster at his age, even his knuckle ball might not want to dance.

Catching is very strong because of the youngster Ellie Rodriguez who everyone knows is a top prospect. At first base it could be Mike "Lefty" Fiore, but don't be surprised if Joe Foy moves there so that Paul Schall can play third. If they don't improvise they will probably make a trade, using one of them as bait. Second base can be handled by Billy Harris and at short it will be either Jerry Adair or Jackie Hernandez. Both could do the job. In fact Adair might also do it at third or second.

In the outfield the team isn't strong. Everyone around from the drafts is young, inexperienced and unproven. Steve Whitaker, Joe Keough and Pat Kelly will be given long looks. If the looks are blurred by Gordon's tears, trades and more money will be his only recourse.

Kansas City Royals: Draft Choices in Order of Selection:

1. Roger Nelson, Pitcher from Baltimore.
2. Joe Foy, Third base from Boston. (Possibly the best player selected in American League draft.)
3. Jim Rooker, Pitcher from N.Y. Yankees. No major league experience but exceptional prospects.
4. Joe Keough, Outfielder from Oakland.
5. Steve Jones, Pitcher from Washington; came up briefly in 1967 and again in 1968. Still very inexperienced.

6. Jon Wardon, Pitcher from Detroit. (Excellent arm.)
7. Ellie Rodriguez, Catcher from N.Y. Yankees. (Excellent potential.)
8. Dave Morehead, Pitcher from Boston. If his arm is right can win.
9. Mike Fiore, First baseman from Baltimore. Also can play outfield. Came up for brief trial at end of '68.
10. Bob Oliver, Outfielder from Minnesota, came up briefly at end of 1968 season. Has good potential.
11. Bill Butler, Pitcher from Detroit. No major league experience through 1968 season.
12. Steve Whitaker, Outfielder from N.Y. Yankees.
13. Wally Bunker, Pitcher from Baltimore.
14. Paul Schall, Third base, from California. (Was hit on skull during 1968 season. Effects not known yet regarding impairment on emotional and mental level.)
15. Bill Haynes, Infielder from Chicago White Sox. No major league experience through 1968 season.
16. Rick Drago, Pitcher from Detroit. No major league experience.
17. Pat Kelly, Outfielder from Minnesota. (Brother Leroy does okay for the Cleveland Browns.)
18. Bill Harris, Second baseman from Cleveland.
19. Don O'Riley, Pitcher from Oakland. No previous major league experience.
20. Al Fitzmorris, Pitcher from Chicago White Sox. No previous major league experience.
21. Moe Drabowsky, Relief Pitcher from Baltimore. (Many teams can use him for pennant fights.)
22. Jackie Hernandez, Shortstop from Minnesota.
23. Hoyt Wilhelm, Relief Pitcher from Chicago White Sox. (Best at his trade in the history of the game, he is a young 45.)
24. Mike Hedlund, Pitcher from Cleveland. Appeared briefly and ineffectually at end of 1968 season.

25. Tom Burgmier, Pitcher from California.
26. Jerry Adair, Multi-talented second and third baseman and shortstop from Boston. (Has to help.)
27. Gerald Cram, Pitcher from Minnesota. No previous major league experience through 1968 season.
28. Fran Healey, Catcher from Cleveland. No major league experience through 1968 season.
29. Scott Northey, Outfielder from Chicago White Sox. No major league experience through 1968 season.
30. Ed Brookens, Pitcher from Washington. No major league experience through 1968 season. (Mr. Brookens can say he was worth $175,000—How about that. . . .)

Seattle Pilots: Manager Joe Schultz

Ex-Cardinal coach Joe Schultz has left the comforts of coaching a team in the middle of greatness to manage the Pilots where he will not fly and we hope not fall. Joe must have seen the Wright brothers once too often or his sense of adventure is just plain overwhelming. He started with some good pitching selections in Gary Bell, Steve Barber, Diego Segui and Jack Aker who can be valuable in relief. After that it is youth and youth and more youth. Some of the best young arms belong to Buzz Stephen and Gerry Schoen. Some of the youth has to mature now if the Pilots are going to get off the ground at all.

Catching will be capably handled by Larry Haney and Gerry McNertney, while it could be the large Don Mincher at first doing a workman-like job. The infield could be fair considering the other positions will have Chico Salmon, Ray Oyler, Rich Rollins and Mike Ferraro for beginners. They can cover all of the grounds, but it's guaranteed they will not fly.

In the outfield he has good protection: yes sir, Joe took what he knows best; two ex-National Leaguers and they're top flight—Tommy Davis and Tommy Harper. Davis was one of the best, and if he puts it all to work can still be one of the best hitters in the game. After all, he's only 29. Look for big years for both Tommys. The other outfielder will probably be Jim Gosger, with Lou Piniella and Wayne Comer given equal rights.

In all, the Pilots might get off the ground. After all, the season is full of scheduled flights from coast to coast. In all, it will be fun, and that is what it's all about. At least that's all it is for the expansion teams. Money has to be in the back seat for these adventurers.

Seattle Pilots Draft Choices in Order of Selection:

1. Don Mincher, First baseman from California.
2. Tommy Harper, Outfielder from Cleveland.
3. Ray Oyler, Shortstop from Detroit.
4. Gerry McNertney, Catcher from Chicago White Sox.
5. Buzz Stephen, Pitcher from Minnesota. Very good potential.
6. Chico Salmon, Infielder from Cleveland.
7. Diego Segui, Pitcher from Oakland.
8. Tommy Davis, Left fielder from Chicago.
9. Marty Pattin, Pitcher from California.
10. Gerald Schoen, Pitcher from Washington. Brought up for brief trial at end of 1968.
11. Gary Bell, Pitcher from Boston.
12. Jack Aker, Relief Pitcher from Oakland.
13. Rich Rollins, Third base, from Minnesota.
14. Lou Piniella, Outfielder, from Cleveland, brought up at end of '68 for brief look.
15. Charles Bates, Pitcher from Washington. No previous major league experience.
16. Larry Haney, Catcher from Baltimore.
17. Dick Baney, Pitcher from Boston. No major league

experience through 1968 season.
18. Steve Hovley, Outfielder, from California. No major league experience through 1968 season.
19. Steve Barber, Pitcher from N.Y. Yankees.
20. John Miklos, Pitcher from Washington. No major league experience through 1968 season.
21. Wayne Comer, Outfielder from Detroit.
22. Darrell Brandon, Pitcher from Boston.
23. Skippy Lockwood, Infielder from Oakland. Major league experience might have been as pinch runner in 1968.
24. Gary Timberlake, Pitcher from N.Y. Yankees. This youngster is only twenty, and just starting to make his left arm do what he wants it to. Not this year, but he has a future. No major league experience.
25. Robert Richmond, Pitcher from Washington. No major league experience.
26. John Morris, Pitcher from Baltimore. (Could be a real sleeper.)
27. Mike Marshall, Pitcher from Detroit.
28. Jim Gosger, Outfielder from Oakland.
29. Mike Ferraro, Third base from N.Y. Yankees. Limited experience as major leaguer. Played briefly in 1967 and '68.
30. Paul Click, Pitcher from California. No previous major league experience.

12

The Comprehensive and Chart Rating of 1969 Player Personnel

On the pages that follow every player who appeared during the past season and who should be playing or has good prospects of playing at this time for a major league team has been considered and evaluated. (*On career performances.*) We have used the six categorical rating system diligently in preparing this chapter. The changes that took place because of trades and other minute changes after the book went to press naturally cannot be included. But we have tried to give you all the up to date information possible in rating each ball player for the 1969 season. The material should provide just this. For the players that entered the league late in '68 or with very little experience we have prepared the following key for you to follow.

KEY: 1969 PLAYER PERSONNEL:
1—player came up at end of 1968 season. Fair potential for 1969 season. Inexperienced.
2—Insufficient evidence to rate through 1968. Excellent prospect for 1969.
3—Less than full year in Major Leagues, potential good. Rating indicates achievements through particular chart scores in individual categoricals.

EXPLANATION OF "FIRST YEAR," OR "FIRST GAME" IN MAJOR LEAGUES:

On the composite listing of 1969 pitchers and players, as well as on the charts the indication for the current (1969) players the heading "first year" or "first game" in major leagues is included. This refers specifically to the first season that the player appeared in a major league game. Therefore the player might have appeared for one game only, and at that only as a pinch runner, hitter, or defensive fielder. The player might have been sent back to the minor leagues for years after this "one time" appearance. Maybe not. If he was sent back many times "official rookie status" as major leaguer was not gained until a year, two, or many years later. We have used this listing in order to give you a greater comprehension of how many years each player has worked to develop his particular skills for the rating he has received at this time.

POSITION
STARTING PITCHER

	First Game in Major Leagues (or Years in Major Leagues)	Team	Offensive Total	Defensive Total	Total Rating
Juan Marichal	1960	S. F. Giants			95
Bob Gibson	1959	St. L. Cardinals			93
Don Drysdale	1956	L. A. Dodgers			86
Jim Bunning	1955	Pit. Pirates			76
Dennis McLain	1964	Det. Tigers			75
Mel Stottlemyre	1964	N. Y. Yankees			74
Dean Chance	1961	Minn. Twins			70
Luis Tiant	1964	Cleve. Indians			70
Jim Maloney	1960	Cin. Reds			69
Fergeson Jenkins	1965	Chicago Cubs			69
Jim Lonborg	1965	Boston Red Sox			69
Gary Peters	1959	Chicago White Sox			67
Camillio Pasqual	1954	Wash. Senators			67
Chris Short	1959	Phila. Phils			66
Tom Seaver	1967	N. Y. Mets			63
Jim Katt	1959	Minn. Twins			62
Bob Veale	1962	Pit. Pirates			60
Sam McDowell	1961	Cleve. Indians			59
Gaylord Perry	1962	S. F. Giants			59
Mickey Lolich	1963	Detroit Tigers			59
Joel Horlen	1961	Chi. White Sox			59
Milt. Pappas	1957	Atlanta Braves			58
Jim Nash	1966	Oakland A's			57
Dave McNally	1963	Baltimore Orioles			57
Nelson Briles	1965	St. L. Cardinals			56
Claude Osteen	1957	L. A. Dodgers			56
Juan Pizarro	1957	Boston Red Sox			55
Mike McCormick	1956	S. F. Giants			55
Ray Sadecki	1960	S. F. Giants			55

POSITION
STARTING PITCHER
(continued)

Name	First Game in Major Leagues (or Years in Major Leagues)	Team	Offensive Total	Defensive Total	Total Rating
Steve Carlton	1965	St. L. Cardinals			55
Tom Phoebus	1966	Baltimore Orioles			55
Earl Wilson	1959	Detroit Tigers			55
Tommy John	1963	Chicago White Sox			54
Jerry Koosman	1967	N.Y. Mets			54
Bill Monbouquette	1958	(FREE AGENT)			52
Pat Jarvis	1966	Atlanta Braves			52
Gary Nolan	1967	Cin. Reds			52
Gary Bell	1958	Seattle Pilots			52
Jim Hardin	1967	Balt. Orioles			52
Al Downing	1961	N.Y. Yankees			52
Bob Bolin	1961	S.F. Giants			51
Jim Merritt	1965	Minn. Twins			50
Ray Culp	1963	Boston Red Sox			50
Jim "Mudcat" Grant	1958	Montreal Expos			49
Sonny Siebert	1964	Cleveland Indians			49
Larry Dierker	1964	Houston Astros			49
Don Wilson	1966	Houston Astros			49
Jose Santiago	1963	Boston Red Sox			49
John "Blue Moon" Odum	1964	Oakland A's			48
Stan Williams	1958	Cleveland Indians			48
Mike Cuellar	1959	Houston Astros			48
Ray Washburn	1961	St. L. Cardinals			48
Stan Bahnsen	1966	N.Y. Yankees			48
Jim "Catfish" Hunter	1965	Oakland A's			48
Steve Blass	1964	Pit. Pirates			48
Don Singer	1964	L.A. Dodgers			47
Denver Lemaster	1962	Houston Astros			47

POSITION
STARTING PITCHER
(continued)

Name	First Game in Major Leagues (or Years in Major Leagues)	Team	Offensive Total	Defensive Total	Total Rating
Al Jackson	1959	N.Y. Mets			47
Bill Hands	1965	Chicago Cubs			47
Ken Holtzman	1965	Chicago Cubs			45
Fritz Peterson	1966	N.Y. Yankees			45
Sammy Ellis	1962	Calif. Angels			45
Ken Johnson	1958	Atlanta Braves			45
Ron Reed	1966	Atlanta Braves			45
Al McBean	1961	San Diego Padres			45
Dick Ellsworth	1960	Boston Red Sox			45
Dave Guisti	1962	San Diego Padres			45
Tony Cloninger	1961	Cin. Reds			45
Joe Coleman	1965	Wash. Senators			45
Jim McGlothlin	1965	Calif. Angels			44
Rick Wise	1964	Phila. Phils			44
George Culver	1966	Cin. Reds			44
Phil Niekro	1964	Atlanta Braves			44
Dave Boswell	1964	Minn. Twins			44
Don Cardwell	1957	N.Y. Mets			44
Joel Niekro	1967	Chicago Cubs			44
Dick Selma	1965	San Diego Padres			44
Lew Krause	1961	Oakland A's			44
Jerry Arrigo	1961	Cin. Reds			44
Woody Fryman	1966	Phila. Phils			43
Nolan Ryan (3)	1966	N.Y. Mets			42
Mike Paul (3)	1968	Cleveland Indians			42
Don Sutton	1966	L.A. Dodgers			42
John Hiller	1965	Detroit Tigers			42
Steve Barber	1960	Seattle Pilots			42

POSITION
STARTING PITCHER
(continued)

	First Game in Major Leagues (or Years in Major Leagues)	Team	Offensive Total	Defensive Total	Total Rating
Steve Hargan	1965	Cleveland Indians			42
Dave Morehead	1963	K.C. Royals			42
Mel Queen Jr.	1966	Cin. Reds			41
Phil Ortega	1960	Wash. Senators			40
Joe Sparma	1964	Detroit Tigers			40
Hank Acquirre	1955	L.A. Dodgers			40
Wally Bunker	1963	K.C. Royals			40
Larry Jaster	1965	Montreal Expos			40
Jack Fisher	1959	Chicago White Sox			40
Pete Richert	1962	Baltimore Orioles			40
Daryl Peterson	1968	Det. Tigers			40
Jim Perry	1959	Minn. Twins			40
George Brunet	1956	Calif. Angels			40
Jim Hannon	1967	Wash. Senators			39
Paul Lindblad	1965	Oakland A's			38
Clyde Wright	1966	Calif. Angels			38
Bob Moose (3)	1967	Pit. Pirates			38
Tom Murphy (3)	1968	Calif. Angels			38
Chuck Dobson	1966	Oakland A's			37
Rich Nye	1966	Chicago Cubs			37
Dick Hughes	1966	St. L. Cardinals			37
Fred Talbot	1963	N.Y. Yankees			37
John O'Donohue	1963	Baltimore Orioles			37
Dave Leonard (3)	1967	Baltimore Orioles			36
Diego Segui	1962	Seattle Pilots			36
Mike Kekich (3)	1965	L.A. Dodgers			36
Jim Ray (3)	1965	Houston Astros			36
Vincente Romo (3)	1968	Cleveland Indians			36

POSITION
STARTING PITCHER
(continued)

	First Game in Major Leagues (or Years in Major Leagues)	Team	Offensive Total	Defensive Total	Total Rating
Joe Verbanic	1966	N.Y. Yankees			34
Barry Moore	1965	Wash. Senators			34
Dennis Bennett	1962	Calif. Angels			33
Francisco Carlos	1967	Chicago White Sox			33
Joe Gibbon	1960	S.F. Giants			33
Tom Hall (3)	1968	Minn. Twins			33
Jim McAndrews (3)	1968	N.Y. Mets			33
Tommy Sisk	1962	Pit. Pirates			32
Gary Waslewski	1967	Boston Red Sox			32
Grant Jackson	1965	Phila. Phils			32
Gary Brabender	1966	Baltimore Orioles			32
Pat Dobson	1967	Detroit Tigers			32
George Stone (3)	1967	Atlanta Braves			32
Dennis Ribant	1964	Chicago White Sox			31
Bruce Howard	1963	Wash. Senators			31
Ricky Clark	1967	Calif. Angels			31
Dick Kelley	1964	San Diego Padres			28
Frank Bertaina	1964	Wash. Senators			27
Wade Blasingame	1963	Houston Astros			27
Bob Priddy	1962	Wash. Senators			27
Danny Frisella (3)	1967	N.Y. Mets			37
Jeff James (3)	1968	Phila. Phils			25
Jim Britton (3)	1967	Atlanta Braves			25
Jerry Johnson (3)	1968	Phila. Phils			25
Jim Roland	1962	Minn. Twins			24
Jerry Stephenson	1963	Boston Red Sox			24
Tony Pierce	1967	Oakland A's			24
Luke Walker	1965	Pit. Pirates			24
Warren Bogle (3)	1968	Oakland A's			24

POSITION
STARTING PITCHER (continued)

Name	First Game in Major Leagues (or Years in Major Leagues)	Team	Offensive Total	Defensive Total	Total Rating
Gary Ross (3)	1968	Chicago Cubs			24
John Lazar (3)	1968	Chicago White Sox			23
Roger Nelson (3)	1967	K. C. Royals			23
Daryl Brandon	1936	Seattle Pilots			23
Horatio Pina (3)	1968	Cleveland Indians			22
John Boozer	1962	Phila. Phils			21
Jon Warden	1968	K. C. Royals			20
Will Harrelson (3)	1968	Angels			19

POSITION
PITCHER

Name	First Game in Major Leagues (or Years in Major Leagues)	Team	Offensive Total	Defensive Total	Total Rating
Players Without Chartered Scores: Rated on Earlier Appearances					
A. Jim Palmer (2)	1965	Baltimore Orioles			52
B. Dave Wickersham (2)	1960	K. C. Royals			40
C. John Tsitoris (2)	1957	N. Y. Yankees			37
D. Jim Bouton	1962	San Diego Padres			37
E. Bob Hendley (2)	1961	N. Y. Mets			33
F. Chuck Estrada	1960	N. Y. Mets			31
G. Joel Moeller (2)	1962	L. A. Dodgers			31

A. Palmer inactive in 1968 because of arm injury. Rating based on previous major league experience. If recuperated prospects excellent.

B. Wickersham in minor leagues in 1968. Rating based on previous major league experience.

C. Tsitoris rating based on previous major league experience, did not participate in majors in 1968.

D. Bouton has opportunity to appear for San Diego Padres in 1969. He was released in middle of '68 season by N. Y. Yankees.

E. Hendley rating based on major league experience through '67 season. In '68 he was mainly in minor leagues.

F. Estrada rating based on major league experience through '67 season. In '68 he was mainly in minor leagues.

G. Moeller rating based on major league experience through 1968. He was brought up again in Sept. and his potential is good.

POSITION
PITCHER

	First Game in Major Leagues (or Years in Major Leagues)	Team	Offensive Total	Defensive Total	Total Rating

Players Without Chartered Scores: No Rating

- A. Jerry Nyman (2) — 1968 — Chicago White Sox
- B. John Cumberland (1) — 1968 — N.Y. Yankees
  - Rick Beck (1) — 1966 — N.Y. Yankees
  - Mike Hedlund (1) — 1968 — K.C. Royals
- C. Frank "Tug" McGraw (2) — 1965 — N.Y. Mets
  - Jim Ollum (2) — 1966 — Minn. Twins
  - Carroll Sembera (1) — 1965 — Houston Astros
  - Chris Zachery (2) — 1966 — Houston Astros
- D. Les Cain (2) — 1968 — Detroit Tigers
  - George Woodson (1) — 1968 — Cleve. Indians
- E. Mike Adamson (2) — 1967 — Baltimore Orioles
- F. Les Rohr (2) — 1967 — N.Y. Mets
  - Archie Reynolds (1) — 1968 — Chicago Cubs
  - Alan Foster (2) — 1967 — L.A. Dodgers
  - Danny Fast (2) — 1968 — Chicago Cubs
  - Bruce Dal Canton (1) — 1967 — Pit. Pirates
  - Rob Gardner (1) — 1965 — Cleve. Indians
- G. Wayne Granger (2) — 1968 — Cin. Reds
  - Jim Miles (1) — 1968 — Wash. Senators
  - Alan Santorini (2) — 1968 — San Diego Padres
  - Ron Keller (1) — 1968 — Minn. Twins
  - Steve Kealey (1) — 1968 — Calif. Angels
  - Bill Wynne (1) — 1967 — Chi. White Sox
- H. Jerry Schoen (2) — 1968 — Seattle Pilots
  - Roland Fingers (1) — 1968 — Oakland A's
  - Steve Bailey (1) — 1967 — Cleve. Indians

POSITION
PITCHER

	First Game in Major Leagues (or Years in Major Leagues)	Team	Offensive Total	Defensive Total	Total Rating

Players Without Chartered Scores: No Rating (continued)

Fred Rath (1)	1968	Chic. White Sox			
Rich Robertson (1)	1966	S. F. Giants			
Dan McGinn (1)	1968	Montreal Expos			
Steve Jones (1)	1967	K. C. Royals			
Danny Morris (1)	1968	Minn. Twins			
Louis "Buzz" Stephen (2)	1968	Seattle Pilots			
Ken Brett (1)	1967	Boston Red Sox			

A. Nyman excellent prospect for 1969.

B. Cumberland inexperienced but very good prospect.

C. McGraw has been in Majors and Minors for past four seasons, should be ready to realize fine potential.

D. Cain has exceptional potential. Very strong arm.

E. Adamson is youngester with excellent potential for 1969 season.

F. Rohr has exceptional arm and if he can harness his control has very good prospects for 1969 season.

G. Granger appeared intermittently for St. L. Cardinals during 1968 season. He showed very strong potential as starter and reliever. Traded to Cincinnati and can be top pitcher.

H. Schoen is a hard thrower and excellent prospect.

STARTING PITCHERS

THE SIX PITCHING CATEGORICALS

Rating Scale in points:	1-TEAM VALUE	2-POWER	3-PITCHING ARSENAL VALUE TECHNICAL PROFICIENCY	4-CONTROL	5-EXPERIENCE	6-VERSATILITY AND EXECUTION	TOTAL POINTS
	25	25	20	20	10	10	110 Max (ideal)
JUAN MARICHAL, 1960, S. F. Giants	19	21	18	20	8	9	95
BOB GIBSON, 1959, St. L. Cardinals	19	19	19	17	10	9	93
DON DRYSDALE, 1956, L. A. Dodgers	17	15	16	19	10	9	86
JIM BUNNING, 1955, Pit. Pirates	14	14	15	16	10	7	76
DENNIS McLAIN, 1964, Det. Tigers	17	16	16	14	6	6	75
MEL STOTTLEMYRE, 1964, N. Y. Yankees	17	13	14	15	7	8	74
DEAN CHANCE, 1961, Minn. Twins	13	15	16	14	7	5	70
LUIS TIANT, 1964, Cleve. Indians	13	12	17	16	5	7	70
JIM MALONEY, 1960, Cinn. Reds	13	15	14	13	7	7	69
FERGUSON JENKINS, 1965, Chicago Cubs	14	14	15	14	6	6	69
JIM LONBORG, 1965, Boston Red Sox	14	13	16	12	6	6	67
GARY PETERS, 1959, Chicago White Sox	12	14	13	13	7	8	67
CAMILLIO PASQUAL, 1954, Wash. Senators	12	10	14	15	9	7	67
CHRIS SHORT, 1959, Phila. Phils	13	12	14	13	7	7	66
TOM SEAVER, 1967, N. Y. Mets	12	14	14	14	2	7	63
JIM KATT, 1959, Minn. Twins	13	10	11	14	6	8	62
BOB VEALE, 1962, Pitt. Pirates	12	14	12	10	7	5	60
SAM MC DOWELL, 1961, Cleve. Indians	11	16	13	8	6	5	59
GAYLORD PERRY, 1962, S. F. Giants	11	12	12	12	6	6	59
JOEL HORLEN, 1961, Chicago White Sox	11	10	12	15	6	5	59

STARTING PITCHERS

THE SIX PITCHING CATEGORICALS

Rating Scale in points:	1-TEAM VALUE	2-POWER	3-PITCHING ARSENAL VALUE TECHNICAL PROFICIENCY	4-CONTROL	5-EXPERIENCE	6-VERSATILITY AND EXECUTION	TOTAL POINTS
	25	25	20	20	10	10	110 Max (ideal)
MICKEY LOLICH, 1963, Det. Tigers	13	13	12	11	5	5	59
MILT PAPPAS, 1957, Atlanta Braves	10	12	11	12	7	6	58
JIM NASH, 1966, Oakland Athletics	11	14	13	10	4	5	57
DAVE McNALLY, 1962, Baltimore Orioles	12	10	12	13	5	5	57
NELSON BRILES, 1965, St. L. Cardinals	11	11	12	12	5	5	56
CLAUDE OSTEEN, 1957, L. A. Dodgers	10	10	10	12	7	7	56
JUAN PIZARRO, 1957, Boston Red Sox	10	11	10	11	7	6	55
MIKE McCORMICK, 1956, S. F. Giants	10	11	10	13	6	5	55
RAY SADECKI, 1960, S. F. Giants	11	13	10	10	5	6	55
STEVE CARLTON, 1965, St. L. Cardinals	9	11	14	13	3	5	55
TOM PHOEBUS, 1966, Balt. Orioles	12	11	14	10	3	5	55
EARL WILSON, 1959, Det. Tigers	10	10	10	10	5	10	55
TOMMY JOHN, 1963, Chicago White Sox	11	11	11	11	5	5	54
JERRY KOOSMAN, 1967, N.Y. Mets	14	8	14	13	1	4	54
BILL MONBOUQUETTE, 1958, *	9	10	10	12	6	5	52
PAT JARVIS, 1966, Atlanta Braves	11	10	11	13	2	5	52
GARY NOLAN, 1967, Cin. Reds	12	8	13	14	1	4	52

*Monbouquette finished 1968 with S. F. Giants. At this time, he is a free agent and seeking to negotiate for major league position.

STARTING PITCHERS

THE SIX PITCHING CATEGORICALS

Rating Scale in points:	1-TEAM VALUE	2-POWER	3-PITCHING ARSENAL VALUE TECHNICAL PROFICIENCY	4-CONTROL	5-EXPERIENCE	6-VERSATILITY AND EXECUTION	TOTAL POINTS
	25	25	20	20	10	10	110 Max (ideal)
JIM HARDIN, 1967, Balt. Orioles	12	10	12	12	2	4	52
AL DOWNING, 1961, N.Y. Yankees	9	9	13	10	5	6	52
GARY BELL, 1958, Seattle Pilots	10	10	10	10	7	5	52
BOB BOLIN, 1961, S. F. Giants	10	10	10	10	6	5	51
JIM MERRITT, 1965, Minn. Twins	10	8	9	15	3	5	50
RAY CULP, 1963, Boston Red Sox	10	9	12	10	4	5	50
"MUD CAT" JIM GRANT, 1958, Montreal Expos	9	9	9	11	6	5	49
SONNY SIEBERT, 1964, Cleve. Indians	9	10	10	10	5	5	49
LARRY DIERKER, 1964, Houston Astros	10	7	12	12	3	5	49
DON WILSON, 1966, Houston Astros	9	9	14	10	2	5	49
JOSE SANTIAGO, 1968, Boston Red Sox	11	8	10	10	5	5	59
STEVE BLASS, 1964, Pitt. Pirates	10	10	10	9	4	5	48
JOHN "BLUE MOON" ODOM, 1964, Oakland Athletics	9	8	13	10	3	5	48
MIKE CUELLAR, 1959, Houston Astros	10	9	9	10	5	5	48
RAY WASHBURN, 1961, St. L. Cardinals	9	10	10	12	3	4	48
STAN BAHNSEN, 1966, N.Y. Yankees	11	10	12	10	1	4	48
JIM "CATFISH" HUNTER, 1965, Oakland Athletics	10	10	10	10	3	5	48
DON SINGER, 1964, L. A. Dodgers	9	8	13	10	2	5	47
DENVER LEMASTER, 1962, Houston Astros	9	9	10	10	4	5	47
BILL HANDS, 1965, Chicago Cubs	10	8	10	12	2	5	47

STARTING PITCHERS

THE SIX PITCHING CATEGORICALS

	1-TEAM VALUE	2-POWER	3-PITCHING ARSENAL VALUE	4-TECHNICAL PROFICIENCY CONTROL	5-EXPERIENCE	6-VERSATILITY AND EXECUTION	TOTAL POINTS
Rating Scale in points:	25	25	20	20	10	10	110 Max (ideal)
AL JACKSON, 1959, N.Y. Mets	8	8	9	10	5	7	47
KEN HOLTZMAN, 1965, Chicago Cubs	8	10	13	8	2	5	46
SAMMY ELLIS, 1962, Calif. Angels	9	10	8	8	6	5	46
KEN JOHNSON, 1958, Atlanta Braves	7	7	10	10	6	5	45
RON REED, 1966, Atlanta Braves	9	8	10	11	2	5	45
AL McBEAN, 1961, San Diego Padres	7	9	9	10	5	5	45
FRITZ PETERSON, 1968, N.Y. Yankees	9	8	9	12	2	5	45
DICK ELLSWORTH, 1960, Boston Red Sox	9	7	9	10	5	5	45
TONY CLONINGER, 1961, Cin. Reds	8	9	12	7	5	4	45
JOE COLEMAN, 1965, Wash. Senators	9	7	11	11	2	5	45
JIM McGLOTHLIN, 1965, Calif. Angels	9	7	12	9	2	5	44
RICK WISE, 1964, Phila Phils	8	8	10	10	3	5	44
GEORGE CULVER, 1966, Cin. Reds	8	8	10	11	2	5	44
PHIL NIEKRO, 1964, Atlanta Braves	8	7	12	10	3	4	44
DAVE BOSWELL, 1964, Minn. Twins	8	9	11	8	2	6	44
DON CARDWELL, 1957, N.Y. Mets	7	6	10	10	6	5	44
JOEL NIEKRO, 1967, Chicago Cubs	8	8	11	11	1	5	44
DICK SELMA, 1965, San Diego Padres	8	8	13	9	2	4	44
LEW KRAUSE, 1961, Oakland Athletics	8	8	8	10	5	5	44
JERRY ARRIGO, 1961, Cin. Reds	8	8	9	9	5	5	44

STARTING PITCHERS

THE SIX PITCHING CATEGORICALS

Rating Scale in points:	1-TEAM VALUE	2-POWER	3-PITCHING ARSENAL VALUE TECHNICAL PROFICIENCY	4-CONTROL	5-EXPERIENCE	6-VERSATILITY AND EXECUTION	TOTAL POINTS
	25	25	20	20	10	10	110 Max (ideal)
WOODY FRYMAN, 1966, Phila. Phils	8	8	10	10	3	4	43
JOHN HILLER, 1967, Det. Tigers	8	5	12	10	2	5	42
NOLAN RYAN, 1966, N.Y. Mets	6	7	16	8	1	4	42
DON SUTTON, 1966, L. A. Dodgers	7	7	10	10	3	5	42
STEVE BARBER, 1960, Seattle Pilots	7	10	10	4	5	6	42
MIKE PAUL, 1968, Cleve. Indians	6	5	15	10	1	5	42
DAVE MOREHEAD, 1963, K. C. Royals	6	7	11	9	4	5	42
MEL QUEEN, JR., 1966, Cin. Reds	6	8	11	9	2	5	41
PHIL ORTEGA, 1960, Washington Senatore	8	8	9	8	4	3	40
JOE SPARMA, 1964, Detroit Tigers	7	7	9	8	4	5	40
HANK ACQUIRRE, 1955, L. A. Dodgers	7	8	8	8	7	2	40
WALLY BUNKER, 1963, K. C. Royals	8	6	9	10	3	4	40
LARRY JASTER, 1965, Montreal Expos	7	8	10	9	2	4	40
JACK FISHER, 1959, Chicago White Sox	7	6	7	10	6	4	40
PETE RICHERT, 1962, Baltimore Orioles	6	8	8	7	6	5	40
DARYL PATTERSON, 1968, Det. Tigers	6	4	12	10	2	6	40
JIM PERRY, 1959, Minn. Twins	6	8	8	9	5	3	39
JIM HANNON, 1967, Wash. Senatore	8	6	8	8	4	5	39
PAUL LINDBLAD, 1965, Oakland Athletics	6	6	8	10	3	5	38
CLYDE WRIGHT, 1966, Calif. Angels	7	5	8	9	4	5	38
BOB MOOSE, 1967, Pitt. Pirates	5	2	12	12	2	5	38

STARTING PITCHERS

THE SIX PITCHING CATEGORICALS

Rating Scale in points:	1-TEAM VALUE	2-POWER	3-PITCHING ARSENAL VALUE	4-CONTROL TECHNICAL PROFICIENCY	5-EXPERIENCE	6-VERSATILITY AND EXECUTION	TOTAL POINTS
	25	25	20	20	10	10	110 Max (ideal)
TOM MURPHY, 1968, Calif. Angels	4	5	11	11	2	5	38
CHUCK DOBSON, 1966, Oakland Athletics	7	6	8	10	2	4	37
RICH NYE, 1966, Chicago Cubs	5	6	8	11	2	5	37
DICK HUGHES, 1966, St. L. Cardinals	7	6	9	7	4	4	37
FRED TALBOT, 1963, N.Y. Yankees	5	6	9	7	5	5	37
JOHN O'DONOHUE, 1963, Balt. Orioles	5	5	8	8	6	5	37
DAVE LEONARD, 1967, Balt. Orioles	7	5	10	8	1	5	36
DIEGO SEQUI, 1962, Seattle Pilots	4	6	7	8	6	5	36
MIKE KEKICH, 1965, L.A. Dodgers	4	2	14	9	2	5	36
JIM RAY, 1965, Houston Astros	4	4	12	10	1	5	36
VINCENTE ROMO, 1968, Cleve. Indians	5	3	11	11	1	5	36
DENNIS BENNETT, 1962, Calif. Angels	5	5	5	10	5	3	35
BARRY MOORE, 1965, Washington	4	4	8	9	3	6	34
JOE VERBANIC, 1966, N.Y. Yankees	5	5	7	7	4	6	34
FRANCISCO CARLOS, 1967, Chicago White Sox	3	5	9	10	1	5	33
JOE GIBBON, 1960, S.F. Giants	4	4	7	7	6	5	33
TOM HALL, 1968, Minn. Twins	0	0	13	13	1	6	33
JIM McANDREWS, 1968, N.Y. Mets	1	1	12	13	0	6	33
TOMMY SISK, 1962, Pitt. Pirates	5	4	6	8	5	4	32
GARY WASLEWSKI, 1967, Boston Red Sox	4	5	7	9	3	4	32

STARTING PITCHERS

THE SIX PITCHING CATEGORICALS

Rating Scale in points:	1-TEAM VALUE	2-POWER	3-PITCHING ARSENAL VALUE TECHNICAL PROFICIENCY	4-CONTROL	5-EXPERIENCE	6-VERSATILITY AND EXECUTION	TOTAL POINTS
	25	25	20	20	10	10	110 Max (ideal)
GRANT JACKSON, 1965, Phila. Phils	3	2	13	8	1	5	32
GARY BRABENDEN 1966, Balt. Orioles	3	3	10	9	2	5	32
PAT DOBSON, 1967, Detroit Tigers	3	4	9	9	2	5	32
GEORGE STONE, 1967, Atl. Braves	2	4	12	9	1	4	32
DENNIS RIBANT, 1964, Chicago White Sox	2	5	6	8	5	5	31
BRUCE HOWARD, 1963, Wash. Senators	4	5	6	5	5	6	31
RICKY CLARKE, 1967, Calif. Angels	5	5	8	7	2	4	31
DICK KELLEY, 1964, San Diego Padres	5	5	5	5	4	4	28
FRANK BERTAINA, 1964, Wash. Senators	3	3	5	9	2	5	27
WADE BLASINGAME, 1963, Houston Astros	4	4	5	5	4	5	27
DANNY FRISELLA, 1967, N.Y. Mets	3	2	9	9	1	3	27
BOB PRIDDY, 1962, Wash. Senators	3	3	6	9	2	4	27
JEFF JAMES, 1968, Phila. Phils	0	2	8	10	0	5	25
JIM BRITTON, 1967, Atlanta Braves	0	2	11	7	0	5	25
JERRY JOHNSON, 1968, Phila. Phils	0	0	10	10	0	5	25
JIM ROLAND, 1962, Minn. Twins	3	3	6	5	3	4	24
JERRY STEPHENSON, 1963, Boston Red Sox	3	4	7	4	2	4	24
TONY PIERE, 1967, Oakland Athletics	0	1	9	9	0	5	24
LUKE WALKER, 1965, Pit. Pirates	1	2	8	7	1	5	24
WARREN BOGLE, 1968, Oakland Athletics	0	0	12	9	0	3	24

STARTING PITCHERS

THE SIX PITCHING CATEGORICALS

Rating Scale in points:	1-TEAM VALUE	2-POWER	3-PITCHING ARSENAL VALUE TECHNICAL PROFICIENCY	4-CONTROL	5-EXPERIENCE	6-VERSATILITY AND EXECUTION	TOTAL POINTS
	25	25	20	20	10	10	110 Max (ideal)
GARY ROSS, 1968, Chicago Cubs	0	0	9	9	1	5	24
JOHN LAZAR, 1968, Chicago White Sox	0	0	9	9	0	5	23
ROGER NELSON, 1967, K. C. Royals	1	1	8	9	1	3	23
DARYL BRANDON, 1966, Seattle Pilots	2	3	5	5	3	5	23
HORATIO PINA, 1968, Cleve. Indians	0	0	10	8	0	4	22
JOHN BOOZER, 1962, Phila. Phils	2	3	5	5	2	4	21
JOHN WARDON, 1968, K. C. Royals	1	1	6	6	1	6	20
WILL HARRELSON, 1968, Calif. Angels	1	1	6	8	0	3	19

POSITION
RELIEF PITCHER

	First Game in Major Leagues (or Years in Major Leagues)	Team	Offensive Total	Defensive Total	Total Rating
Hoyt Wilhelm	1952	K. C. Royals			64
Elroy Face	1953	Detroit Tigers			62
Frank Linzy	1963	S. F. Giants			57
Dick Hall	1955	Phila. Phils			55
Don McMahon	1957	Detroit Tigers			54
John Wyatt	1961	Detroit Tigers			54
Lindy McDaniel	1955	N. Y. Yankees			54
Ted Abernathy	1955	Cin. Reds			52
Phil Regan	1960	Chicago Cubs			51
Moe Drabowski	1956	K. C. Royals			50
Ron Perranoski	1961	Minn. Twins			49
Ron Kline	1952	Pit. Pirates			48
Joel Hoerner	1963	St. L. Cardinals			48
Al Worthington	1953	Minn. Twins			47
Minnie Rojas	1966	Calif. Angels			44
Bill McCool	1964	San Diego Padres			44
Ed Watt	1966	Baltimore Orioles			44
Claude Raymond	1959	Atlanta Braves			44
Jack Aker	1964	Seattle Pilots			44
Bob Locker	1965	Chicago White Rox			41
Steve Hamilton	1961	N. Y. Yankees			41
Ron Taylor	1962	N. Y. Mets			41
Wilbur Wood	1961	Chicago White Sox			40
Ron Willis	1966	St. L. Cardinals			39
Ed Fisher	1959	Calif. Angels			38
Cal Koonce	1962	N. Y. Mets			38
Cecil Upshaw	1966	Atlanta Braves			38
John Billingham	1968	Montreal Expos			38

**POSITION
RELIEF PITCHER
(continued)**

	First Game in Major Leagues (or Years in Major Leagues)	Team	Offensive Total	Defensive Total	Total Rating
Darold Knowles	1965	Wash. Senators			37
John Purdin	1968	L. A. Dodgers			37
Clay Carroll	1964	Cin. Reds			37
John Buzhardt	1958	Houston Astros			36
Dick Farrell	1956	Phila. Phils			34
Bob Miller	1957	Minn. Twins			34
Jim Brewer	1960	L. A. Dodgers			34
Dennis Higgins	1966	Wash. Senators			33
Pete Mikelson	1964	L. A. Dodgers			33
Gary Wagner (A)	1965	Phila. Phils			30
Lee Stange	1961	Boston Red Sox			30
Jack Hamilton	1962	Cleveland Indians			30
Bill Landis	1963	Boston Red Sox			30
Fred Gladding	1961	Houston Astros			29
Doolie Womack	1966	N. Y. Yankees			25
Jay Ritchie	1964	Cin. Reds			25
Orlando Pena	1958	Cleve. Indians			25
Sparky Lyle	1967	Boston Red Sox			24
Fred Lasher	1963	Detroit Tigers			24
Marty Pattin	1968	Seattle Pilots			23
Bob Lee	1964	Cin. Reds			23
Bill Kelso	1964	Cin. Reds			22
Ed Sprague	1968	Oakland A's			22
Bill Short	1960	N. Y. Mets			21
Bob Humphreys	1962	Wash. Senators			21
Don Shaw (3)	1967	Montreal Expos			20
Andy Messersmith (3) (B)	1968	Calif. Angels			19
Chuck Hartenstein	1966	Chicago Cubs			19

**POSITION
RELIEF PITCHER
(Continued)**

	First Game in Major Leagues (or Years in Major Leagues)	Team	Offensive Total	Defensive Total	Total Rating
Dave Baldwin	1966	Wash. Senators			19
Jack Lamabe	1962	Chicago Cubs			17
Ted Davidson	1965	Atlanta Braves			17
Bill Connors (3)	1967	N. Y. Mets			17
Bill Stoneman	1967	Montreal Expos			17
John Morris	1965	Seattle Pilots			17
Larry Bearnarth (C)	1963	N. Y. Mets			17
Mel Nelson	1960	St. L. Cardinals			17
Casey Cox	1966	Wash. Senators			16
Bill Rohr	1967	Cleve. Indians			13
Thad Tillotson	1967	N. Y. Yankees			11
Tom Dukes	1967	San Diego Padres			9
Danny Coombs	1963	Houston Astros			9
Pat House	1967	Houston Astros			8
Tom Burgmier (3)	1968	K. C. Royals			7
Ken Sanders (3)	1964	Oakland A's			6
Hal Kurtz (3)	1968	Cleve. Indians			0
Steve Shea (2)	1968	Houston Astros			0
Mike Marshall (2)	1967	Seattle Pilots			0
Skip Guinn (1)	1968	Montreal Expos			0

A. Wagner came back to league in 1968 after recovering from bad arm. With health, prospects excellent.

B. Messersmith used mainly as reliever in 1968 but also has good potential as starter.

C. Bearnath rating based on previous major league experience.

RELIEF PITCHERS

THE SIX PITCHING CATEGORICALS

Rating Scale in points:	1-TEAM VALUE	2-POWER	3-PITCHING ARSENAL VALUE TECHNICAL PROFICIENCY	4-CONTROL	5-EXPERIENCE	6-VERSATILITY AND EXECUTION	TOTAL POINTS
	15	15	10	10	10	10	70 Max (ideal)
HOYT WILHELM, 1952, K.C. Royals	15	15	10	8	10	6	64
ELROY FACE, 1953, Detroit Tigers	12	15	10	8	10	7	62
FRANK LINZY, 1963, S.F. Giants	14	14	10	8	5	6	57
DICK HALL, 1955, Phila. Phils	10	12	8	10	10	5	55
DON McMAHON, 1957, Detroit Tigers	11	12	7	8	10	6	54
JOHN WYATT, 1961, Detroit Tigers	12	12	8	6	10	6	54
LINDY McDANIEL, 1955, N.Y. Yankees	11	11	9	7	10	6	54
TED ABERNATHY, 1955, Cin. Reds	12	11	10	8	6	5	52
PHIL REGAN, 1956, Chicago Cubs	11	11	9	8	6	6	51
MOE DRABOWSKI, 1956, K.C. Royals	11	11	8	8	6	6	50
RON PERRANOSKI, 1961, Minn. Twins	11	12	8	7	6	5	49
RONNIE KLINE, 1952, Pit, Pirates	10	9	7	8	8	6	48
JOEL HOERNER, 1963, St. L. Cardinals	10	10	8	8	6	6	48
AL WORTHINGTON, 1953, Minn. Twins	9	10	9	7	7	5	47
MINNIE ROJAS, 1966, Calif. Angels	9	8	7	9	5	6	44
ED WATT, 1966, Balt. Orioles	10	8	9	8	4	5	44
CLAUDE RAYMOND, 1959, Atlanta Braves	8	8	8	8	6	6	44
JACK AKER, 1964, Seattle Pilots	9	9	8	8	5	5	44'
BILLY McCOOL, 1964, San Diego Padres	10	10	8	5	5	6	44
BOB LOCKER, 1965, Chicago White Sox	9	7	8	7	5	5	41

RELIEF PITCHERS

THE SIX PITCHING CATEGORICALS

Rating Scale in points:	1-TEAM VALUE	2-POWER	3-PITCHING ARSENAL VALUE TECHNICAL PROFICIENCY	4-CONTROL	5-EXPERIENCE	6-VERSATILITY AND EXECUTION	TOTAL POINTS
	15	15	10	10	10	10	70 Max (ideal)
RON TAYLER, 1962, N.Y. Mets	8	8	6	7	7	5	41
STEVE HAMILTON, 1961, N.Y. Yankees	8	8	5	8	7	5	41
WILBUR WOOD, 1961, Chicago White Sox	9	8	7	6	5	5	40
RON WILLIS, 1966, St. L. Cards.	9	7	6	7	5	5	39
ED FISHER, 1959, Calif. Angels	7	8	6	6	6	5	38
CECIL UPSHAW, 1966, Atlanta Braves	7	7	9	7	2	6	38
JOHN BILLINGHAM, 1968, Montreal Expos	8	7	9	7	2	5	38
CAL KOONCE, 1964, N.Y. Mets	8	7	6	7	5	5	38
DAROLD KNOWLES, 1965, Washington Senators	7	7	6	7	5	5	37
JOHN PURDIN, 1968, L.A. Dodgers	8	7	9	7	1	5	37
CLAY CARROLL, 1964, Cin. Reds	8	8	6	5	5	5	37
JOHN BUZHARDT, 1958, Houston Astros	6	5	5	8	7	5	36
DICK FARRELL, 1956, Phila. Phils	6	7	6	5	5	5	34
BOB MILLER, 1957, Minn. Twins	7	7	5	5	6	4	34
JIM BREWER, 1960, L.A. Dodgers	7	6	5	6	5	5	34
DENNIS HIGGINS, 1966, Wash. Senators	7	4	7	7	3	5	33
PETE MIKELSON, 1964, L.A. Dodgers	6	5	6	6	5	5	33
GARY WAGNER, 1956, Phila. Phils	2	4	7	8	4	5	30
JACK HAMILTON, 1962, Cleve. Indians	6	5	7	3	4	5	30
LEE STANGE, 1962, Boston Red Sox	4	4	4	6	7	5	30

RELIEF PITCHERS

THE SIX PITCHING CATEGORICALS

Rating Scale in points:	1-TEAM VALUE	2-POWER	3-PITCHING ARSENAL VALUE TECHNICAL PROFICIENCY	4-CONTROL	5-EXPERIENCE	6-VERSATILITY AND EXECUTION	TOTAL POINTS
	15	15	10	10	10	10	70 Max (ideal)
BILL LANDIS, 1963, Boston Red Sox	7	6	5	5	2	5	30
FRED GLADDING, 1961, Houston Astros	5	5	5	4	5	5	29
DOOLIE WOMACK, 1966, N.Y. Yankees	3	3	4	7	3	5	25
JAY RITCHIE, 1964, Cin. Reds	3	3	4	6	4	5	25
SPARKY LYLES, 1967, Boston Red Sox	4	2	5	5	2	6	24
FRED LASHER, 1963, Detroit Tigers	4	4	5	5	1	5	24
MARTY PATTIN, 1968, Seattle Pilots	4	2	6	6	1	4	23
BOB LEE, 1964, Cin, Reds	3	3	6	2	5	4	23
BILL KELSO, 1964, Cin. Reds	2	3	3	6	3	5	22
ED SPRAGUE, 1968, Oakland Athletics	2	3	5	7	0	5	22
BILL SHORT, 1960, N.Y. Mets	3	1	3	7	2	5	21
BOB HUMPHRIES, 1962, Wash. Senators	3	2	3	5	3	5	21
DON SHAW, 1967, Montreal Expos.	1	1	4	8	1	5	20
ANDY MESSERSMITH, 1968, Calif. Angels	2	2	5	5	1	4	19
CHUCK HARTENSTEIN, 1966, Chicago Cubs	2	2	4	5	1	5	19
DAVE BALDWIN, 1966, Wash. Senators	2	2	4	5	2	4	19
JACK LAMABE, 1962, Chicago Cubs	1	2	3	3	3	5	17
TED DAVIDSON, 1965, Atlanta Braves	2	2	2	4	3	4	17
MEL NELSON, 1960, St. L. Cards	2	1	3	3	4	4	17
BILL CONNORS, 1967, Chicago Cubs	1	1	3	6	1	5	17

RELIEF PITCHERS

THE SIX PITCHING CATEGORICALS

Rating Scale in points:	1-TEAM VALUE	2-POWER	3-PITCHING ARSENAL VALUE TECHNICAL PROFICIENCY	4-CONTROL	5-EXPERIENCE	6-VERSATILITY AND EXECUTION	TOTAL POINTS
	15	15	10	10	10	10	70 Max (ideal)
BILL STONEMAN, 1967, Montreal Expos	1	2	4	5	1	4	17
JOHN MORRIS, 1965, Seattle Pilots	0	2	5	4	1	5	17
CASEY COX, 1966, Wash. Senators	0	1	5	5	0	5	16
BILL ROHR, 1967, Cleve. Indians	0	0	5	4	0	4	13
THAD TILLOTSON, 1967, N.Y. Yankees	0	0	2	4	2	3	11
TOM DUKES, 1967, San Diego Padres	0	1	3	3	1	1	9
DANNY COOMBS, 1963, Houston Astros	0	0	3	3	1	2	9
PAT HOUSE, 1967, Houston Astros	0	0	3	2	1	2	8
TOM BURGHMIER, 1968, K.C. Royals	0	0	3	4	0	0	7
KEN SANDERS, 1964, Oakland Athletics	0	0	3	3	0	0	6

POSITION CATCHER

	First Game in Major Leagues (or Years in Major Leagues)	Team	Offensive Total	Defensive Total	Total Rating
Tim McCarver	1959	St. L. Cards.	57	52	109
Bill Freehan	1961	Detroit Tigers	54	51	105
Johnny Bench	1967	Cin. Reds	52	52	104
Joe Torre	1960	Atl. Braves	62	38	100
Tom Haller	1961	L. A. Dodgers	48	47	95
Randy Hundley	1964	Chi. Cubs	42	45	87
Dwayne Josephson	1965	Chi. White Sox	44	43	87
Jerry Grote	1963	N. Y. Mets	41	46	87
John Roseboro	1957	Minn. Twins	38	45	83
Andy Etchebarren	1962	Balt. Orioles	37	44	81
Jake Gibbs	1962	N. Y. Yankees	39	42	81
Jose Azcue	1960	Cleve. Indians	44	37	81
John Edwards	1961	Houston Astros	41	37	78
Bob Rodgers	1961	Calif. Angels	38	37	75
Clay Dalrymple	1960	Phila. Phils	36	39	75
Paul Casonova	1965	Wash. Senators	33	41	74
J. C. Martin	1959	N. Y. Mets	33	39	72
Duke Sims	1964	Cleve. Indians	38	33	71
John Bateman	1963	Montreal Expos	36	33	69
Jerry May	1964	Pit. Pirates	31	38	69
Tom Satriano	1961	Calif. Angels	36	31	67
Jim French	1965	Wash. Senators	31	34	65
Jack Hiatt	1964	S. F. Giants	38	27	65
Dick Dietz	1966	S. F. Giants	35	29	64
Don Pavletich	1957	Cin. Reds	38	25	63
Elrod Hendricks (3) (A)	1968	Balt. Orioles	34	28	62
Frank Fernandez	1967	N. Y. Yankees	27	35	62
Jim Pagliaroni	1955	Oakland A's	30	31	61

POSITION
CATCHER
(continued)

	First Game in Major Leagues (or Years in Major Leagues)	Team	Offensive Total	Defensive Total	Total Rating
Russ Nixon	1957	Boston Red Sox	32	29	61
Dave Duncan (3)	1967	Oakland A's	29	29	58
Phil Roof	1964	Oakland A's	16	40	56
Bruce Look (3)	1968	Minn. Twins	27	29	56
Gene Oliver	1959	Chicago Cubs	32	22	54
Jim Price	1967	Detroit Tigers	26	27	53
John Gibson	1967	Boston Red Sox	18	34	52
Jeff Torborg	1964	L. A. Dodgers	25	27	52
Dave Ricketts	1963	St. L. Cardinals	22	29	51
Gerry McNertney	1964	Seattle Pilots	20	31	51
Dave Adlesh	1963	St. L. Cardinals	20	30	50
Mike Ryan	1964	Phila. Phils	17	31	48
Ron Brand	1963	Montreal Expos	20	25	45
Eliseo Rodrigues (3) (B)	1968	K. C. Royals	17	27	44
Bob Tillman	1962	Atlanta Braves	22	18	40
Hal King (3) (C)	1967	Houston Astros	17	20	37
Larry Haney	1966	Seattle Pilots	16	20	36
Bill Bryan	1961	Wash. Senators	19	16	35
Bob Barton	1965	S. F. Giants	12	22	34
Pat Corrales	1964	Cin. Reds	13	20	33
Jerry Zimmerman	1961	Minn. Twins	2	29	31
Chris Canizzaro	1965	Pit. Pirates	6	25	31
Carl Taylor (3)	1968	Pit. Pirates	10	20	30
Ken Suarez (3)	1966	Cleve. Indians	6	22	28
Players with Uncharted Scores					
Orlando McFarlene (1)	1967	Calif. Angels			0
Tom Egan (1)	1965	Calif. Angels			0
Manuel Sanguillen (1)	1967	Pit. Pirates			0
Ray Fosse (2) (D)	1967	Cleve. Indians			0

POSITION
CATCHER
(continued)

	First Game in Major Leagues (or Years in Major Leagues)	Team	Offensive Total	Defensive Total	Total Rating
Bill Plummer (1)	1968	Chicago Cubs			0
Randy Bobb (1)	1968	Chicago Cubs			0
John Felske (1)	1968	Chicago Cubs			0
Leon McFadden (1) (E)	1968	Houston Astros			0
George Mitterwald (1)	1966	Minn. Twins			0
Duffy Dyer (1)	1968	N.Y. Mets			0
Jerry Mosses (1)	1965	Boston Red Sox			0
Jim Campanis (1)	1966	L. A. Dodgers			0
Ted Simmons (2) (F)	1968	St. L. Cardinals			0
Walt Hriniak (1)	1968	Atlanta Braves			0
John Boccabella (G)	1963	Montreal Expos			0

A. Hendricks played regularly at end of season, and showed exceptional potential.

B. Rodriquez has good potential.

C. King has excellent potential.

D. One of the best prospects in Cleveland's farm system is Mr. Fosse.

E. McFadden also can play Second base and shortstop.

F. Simmons is best prospect in St. Louis Cardinal organization. He is one of the best prospects in all of minor leagues.

G. Boccabella in minor's in 1968. Also plays first base.

POSITION RATED: CATCHERS

	OFFENSIVE CATEGORICALS							DEFENSIVE CATEGORICALS							
	1-TEAM VALUE	2-POWER	3-TECHNICAL PROFICIENCY	4-SPEED	5-EXPERIENCE	6-VERSATILITY AND EXECUTION	THE OFFENSIVE TOTALS	1-TEAM VALUE	2-POWER	3-TECHNICAL PROFICIENCY	4-SPEED	5-EXPERIENCE	6-VERSATILITY AND EXECUTION	THE DEFENSIVE TOTALS	TOTAL POINTS OF PLAYER
Rating Scale in points:	25	25	25	10	10	10	105 Max	20	10	10	10	10	10	70	175 Max (ideal)
Tim McCarver, 1959, St. L. Cards.	13	12	13	7	6	6	57	13	8	8	8	7	8	52	109
Bill Freehan, 1961, Det. Tigers	13	13	13	5	5	5	54	14	8	8	7	6	8	51	105
John Bench, 1967, Cin. Reds	13	13	13	6	2	5	52	14	9	9	9	2	9	52	104
Joe Torre, 1960, Atl. Braves	16	15	14	4	8	5	62	10	5	5	5	7	6	38	100
Tom Haller, 1961, L. A. Dodgers	11	13	9	5	5	5	48	13	7	7	6	7	7	47	95
Randy Hundley, 1964, Chi. Cubs	9	9	10	5	4	5	42	13	7	7	7	4	7	45	87
Dwayne Josephson, 1965, Chi. Whitesox	11	10	10	5	4	4	44	11	7	7	7	4	7	43	87
Jerry Grote, 1963, N. Y. Mets	8	8	10	6	4	5	41	12	7	7	8	5	7	46	87
John Rosboro, 1957, Minn. Twins	7	7	8	5	6	5	38	11	7	7	6	7	7	45	83
Andy Etcheberren, 1962, Balt. Orio.	8	7	8	6	4	4	37	11	7	7	8	4	7	44	81
Jake Gibbs, 1962, N. Y. Yankees	8	8	8	6	5	4	39	10	7	7	7	5	6	42	81
Jose Azcue, 1960, Cleve. Indians	10	11	10	4	4	5	44	11	6	5	5	5	5	37	81
John Edwards, 1961, Houst. Astros	8	9	10	5	5	4	41	8	6	6	6	5	6	37	78
Bob Rodgers, 1961, Calif. Angels	8	7	9	5	5	4	38	8	6	6	6	5	6	37	75
Clay Dalrymple, 1960, Phila. Phils	7	8	8	5	5	3	36	10	6	6	6	5	6	39	75
Paul Casonova, 1965, Wash. Sen.	7	7	7	5	4	3	33	7	8	8	7	4	7	41	74
J. C. Martin 1959, N. Y. Mets	8	6	8	3	5	3	33	9	6	6	6	6	6	39	72
Duke Sims, 1964, Cleve. Indians	8	9	9	4	4	4	38	9	5	5	5	4	5	33	71

POSITION RATED: CATCHERS (continued)

	OFFENSIVE CATEGORICALS							DEFENSIVE CATEGORICALS							
	1-TEAM VALUE	2-POWER	3-TECHNICAL PROFICIENCY	4-SPEED	5-EXPERIENCE	6-VERSATILITY AND EXECUTION	THE OFFENSIVE TOTALS	1-TEAM VALUE	2-POWER	3-TECHNICAL PROFICIENCY	4-SPEED	5-EXPERIENCE	6-VERSATILITY AND EXECUTION	THE DEFENSIVE TOTALS	TOTAL POINTS OF PLAYER
Rating Scale in points:	25	25	25	10	10	10	105 Max	20	10	10	10	10	10	70	175 Max (ideal)
Jerry May, 1964, Pit. Pirates	7	5	6	5	4	4	31	9	6	6	6	5	6	38	69
John Bateman, 1963, Mont. Expos	8	9	8	2	5	4	36	9	5	5	4	5	5	33	69
Tom Satriano, 1961, Calif. Angels	7	8	9	4	4	4	36	7	5	5	4	5	5	31	67
Jim French, 1965, Wash. Sen.	8	4	8	5	2	4	31	8	6	6	6	2	6	34	65
Jack Hiatt, 1964, S.F. Giants	9	8	10	4	3	4	38	7	4	4	4	3	5	27	65
Dick Dietz, 1966, S.F. Giants	7	6	10	5	2	5	35	7	5	5	5	2	5	29	64
Don Pavletich, 1957, Cin. Reds	4	10	10	4	5	5	38	4	4	4	5	4	4	25	63
Elrod Hendricks, 1968, Balt. Orio.	8	8	9	5	2	4	36	5	5	5	5	2	4	26	62
Frank Fernandez, 1967, N.Y. Yanks.	6	5	7	4	2	3	27	6	7	7	6	2	7	35	62
Jim Pagliaroni, 1955, Oak. A's	5	8	8	0	8	1	30	5	5	5	5	6	5	31	61
Russ Nixon, 1957, Bos. Red Sox	4	5	8	4	5	6	32	4	5	5	5	5	5	29	61
Dave Duncan, 1967, Oakland A's	7	6	7	4	2	3	29	6	5	5	5	3	5	29	58
Phil Roof, 1964, Oakland A's	2	2	4	2	4	2	16	5	8	8	6	6	7	40	56
Bruce Look, 1968, Minn. Twins	6	3	9	4	2	3	27	4	6	6	6	2	5	29	56
Gene Oliver, 1959, Chicago Cubs	8	8	7	2	5	2	32	4	3	3	2	5	5	22	54
Jim Price, 1967, Det. Tigers	5	5	8	4	1	3	26	5	5	5	5	2	5	27	53
John Gibson, 1967, Bos. Red Sox	2	3	5	3	3	2	18	3	7	7	6	5	6	34	52
Jeff Torborg, 1964, L.A. Dodgers	5	3	7	4	3	3	25	4	5	5	5	3	5	27	52

POSITION RATED: CATCHERS (continued)

	OFFENSIVE CATEGORICALS							DEFENSIVE CATEGORICALS							
	1-TEAM VALUE	2-POWER	3-TECHNICAL PROFICIENCY	4-SPEED	5-EXPERIENCE	6-VERSATILITY AND EXECUTION	THE OFFENSIVE TOTALS	1-TEAM VALUE	2-POWER	3-TECHNICAL PROFICIENCY	4-SPEED	5-EXPERIENCE	6-VERSATILITY AND EXECUTION	THE DEFENSIVE TOTALS	TOTAL POINTS OF PLAYER
Rating Scale in points:	25	25	25	10	10	10	105 Max	20	10	10	10	10	10	70	175 Max (ideal)
Dave Ricketts, 1963, St. L. Cards.	3	4	7	4	2	2	22	4	6	6	5	3	5	29	51
Gerry McNertney, 1964, Seattle Pil.	3	3	5	3	4	2	20	3	6	6	5	6	5	31	51
Dave Adlesh, 1963, St. L. Cards.	4	2	6	3	2	3	20	5	6	6	5	3	5	30	50
Mike Ryan, 1964, Phil. Phils	2	2	4	4	3	2	17	2	7	7	6	3	6	31	48
Ron Brand, 1963, Mont. Expos															
Eliseo Rodriquez (3), 1969, K. C. Roy.	0	2	8	4	0	3	17	0	7	7	7	0	6	27	44
Bob Tillman, 1962, Atl. Braves	4	3	6	2	5	2	22	3	3	3	3	3	3	18	40
Hal King (3), 1967, Hous. Astros	0	0	9	4	0	4	17	0	5	5	5	0	5	20	37
Larry Haney, 1966, Seattle Pilots	2	1	6	4	0	3	16	0	5	5	5	0	5	20	36
Bill Bryan, 1961, Wash. Senators	4	3	6	2	2	2	19	2	3	3	3	2	3	16	35
Bob Barton, 1965, S. F. Giants	0	1	6	3	0	2	12	2	3	5	5	2	5	22	34
Pat Corrales, 1964, Cin. Reds	0	3	5	3	0	2	13	0	5	5	5	0	5	20	33
Jerry Zimmerman, 1961, Minn. Tw.	0	0	1	0	1	0	2	4	5	5	5	5	5	29	31
Chris Cannizarro, 1965, Pit. Pir.	0	0	2	2	0	2	6	0	6	6	6	2	5	25	31
Carl Taylor, (3), 1968, Pit. Pir.	0	0	6	2	0	2	10	0	3	5	5	2	5	20	30
Ken Suarez (3), 1966, Cleve. Ind.	0	0	2	2	1	1	6	1	3	6	5	2	5	22	28

**POSITION
FIRST BASE**

	First Game in Major Leagues (or Years in Major Leagues)	Team	Offensive Total	Defensive Total	Total Rating
Orlando Cepeda	1958	St. L. Cardinals	70	52	122
Willie McCovey	1959	S. F. Giants	67	38	105
Harmon Killebrew	1954	Minn. Twins	67	37	104
Norm Cash	1958	Detroit Tigers	52	38	90
Donn Clendennon	1961	Montreal Expos	43	47	90
John "Boog" Powell	1961	Balt. Orioles	55	34	89
George Scott	1966	Boston Red Sox	34	54	88
Rusty Staub	1963	Houston Astros	53	35	88
Joe Pepitone (A)	1962	N. Y. Yankees	44	43	87
Lee May	1965	Cin. Reds	49	38	87
Wes Parker	1964	L. A. Dodgers	35	50	85
Tom Mc Graw	1963	Chi. White Sox	38	43	81
Tito Francona	1956	Atlanta Braves	44	37	81
Ed Kranepool	1962	N. Y. Mets	37	44	81
Fred Whitfield	1962	Cin. Reds	43	34	77
Lee Thomas	1961	Houston Astros	43	34	77
Don Mincher	1960	Seattle Pilots	42	34	76
Danny Cater	1964	Oakland A's	40	35	75
Tony Horton	1964	Cleve. Indians	41	34	75
Ramon Webster	1967	Oakland A's	36	36	72
Rich Reese	1964	Minn. Twins	28	38	66
Dick Nen	1963	Chicago Cubs	29	32	61
John Briggs (B)	1964	Phila. Phils	35	26	61
Mike Epstein	1966	Wash. Senators	33	27	60
Gary Holman (3)	1968	Wash. Senators	25	18	43
Ricardo Joseph (3)	1964	Phila. Phils	19	22	41
Greg Goosen (3)	1965	N. Y. Mets	19	14	33

A. & B. Both Pepitone and Briggs also play capably as outfielders.

POSITION
FIRST BASE

	First Game in Major Leagues (or Years in Major Leagues)	Team	Offensive Total	Defensive Total	Total Rating
Players Without Charted Scores					
Bill Davis (2)	1965	San Diego Padres			
Bob Chance (2)	1963	Wash. Senators			
Clarence Jones (2)	1967	Chicago Cubs			
Chuck Harrison (2) (A)	1966	Houston Astros			
Bob Robertson (2) (B)	1966	Pit. Pirates			
Tony Solaita (1) (C)	1968	N. Y. Yankees			
Mike Hegan (2)	1964	N. Y. Yankees			
Gail Hopkins (1)	1968	Chicago White Sox			
Mike Jorgensen (1)	1968	N. Y. Mets			
James Spencer (1)	1968	Calif. Angels			
Russ Nagelson (1)	1968	Cleve. Indians			
Joe Hague (1)	1968	St. L. Cardinals			
Mike "Lefty" Fiore (D) (1)	1968	K. C. Royals			
Bob Christian (1) (E)	1968	Detroit Tigers			
Rich Hebner (1) (F)	1968	Pit. Pirates			
Nate Colbert (2) (G)	1966	San Diego Padres			

A. Harrison excellent prospect for 1969 season.

B. Robertson exceptional prospect in Pittsburgh farm system.

C. Solaita very inexperienced but best prospect in Yankee Organization.

D. Fiore also plays outfield.

E. Christian also plays third base.

F. Hebner is excellent prospect and also plays third base.

G. Colbert also can be positioned in outfield.

POSITION RATED: FIRST BASE

	OFFENSIVE CATEGORICALS							DEFENSIVE CATEGORICALS							
Rating Scale in points:	1-TEAM VALUE	2-POWER	3-TECHNICAL PROFICIENCY	4-SPEED	5-EXPERIENCE	6-VERSATILITY AND EXECUTION	THE OFFENSIVE TOTALS	1-TEAM VALUE	2-POWER	3-TECHNICAL PROFICIENCY	4-SPEED	5-EXPERIENCE	6-VERSATILITY AND EXECUTION	THE DEFENSIVE TOTALS	TOTAL POINTS OF PLAYER
	25	25	25	10	10	10	105 Max	20	10	10	10	10	10	70	175 Max (ideal)
Orlando Cepeda, 1958, St. L. Cards	16	16	17	4	10	7	70	14	7	7	7	10	7	52	122
Willie McCovey, 1959, S. F. Giants	15	17	16	4	10	5	67	10	5	5	5	8	5	38	105
Harmon Killebrew, 1954, Minn. Tw.	16	20	15	3	10	3	67	10	5	5	4	8	5	37	104
Norm Cash, 1958, Det. Tigers	11	14	12	5	5	5	52	10	6	6	5	6	5	38	90
Donn Clendenon, 1961, Mont. Expos	9	9	10	6	5	4	43	13	7	7	8	5	7	47	90
John "Boog" Powell, 1961, Balt. Or.	13	15	13	4	7	3	55	9	5	5	5	5	5	34	89
George Scott, 1966, Bos. Red Sox	7	9	7	4	4	3	34	14	9	9	9	4	9	54	88
Rusty Staub, 1963, Hous. Astros	13	10	13	5	5	7	53	10	5	6	5	4	5	35	88
Joe Pepitone, 1962, N. Y. Yankees	10	10	10	5	5	4	44	10	7	7	6	6	7	43	87
Lee May, 1965, Cin. Reds	12	11	13	5	3	5	49	10	6	7	6	3	6	38	87
Wes Parker, 1964, L. A. Dodgers	5	7	7	7	4	5	35	12	8	8	8	5	9	50	85
Tom McGraw, 1963, Chi. White Sox	8	8	8	5	4	5	38	11	6	6	8	5	7	43	81
Tito Francona, 1956, Atl. Braves	10	8	11	4	6	5	44	10	5	5	5	6	6	37	81
Ed Kranepool, 1962, N. Y. Mets	9	8	9	3	4	4	37	12	7	7	6	5	7	44	81
Fred Whitfield, 1962, Cin. Reds	10	10	10	4	5	4	43	10	5	5	4	5	5	34	77
Lee Thomas, 1961, Hous. Astros	10	10	10	4	5	4	43	8	5	5	5	5	6	34	77
Don Mincher, 1960, Seattle Pilots	9	10	10	4	5	4	42	9	5	5	5	5	5	34	76
Danny Cater, 1964, Oakland A's	10	8	9	4	5	4	40	9	5	5	5	5	6	35	75
Tony Horton, 1964, Cleve. Ind.	9	9	10	5	4	4	41	10	5	5	5	4	5	34	75

POSITION RATED: FIRST BASE (continued)

	OFFENSIVE CATEGORICALS							DEFENSIVE CATEGORICALS							
	1-TEAM VALUE	2-POWER	3-TECHNICAL PROFICIENCY	4-SPEED	5-EXPERIENCE	6-VERSATILITY AND EXECUTION	THE OFFENSIVE TOTALS	1-TEAM VALUE	2-POWER	3-TECHNICAL PROFICIENCY	4-SPEED	5-EXPERIENCE	6-VERSATILITY AND EXECUTION	THE DEFENSIVE TOTALS	TOTAL POINTS OF PLAYER
Rating Scale in points:	25	25	25	10	10	10	105 Max	20	10	10	10	10	10	70	175 Max (ideal)
Ramon Webster, 1967, Oakland A's	8	7	9	5	3	4	36	8	6	6	6	4	6	36	72
Rich Reese, 1964, Minn. Twins	5	5	8	4	2	4	28	10	6	6	5	5	6	38	66
John Briggs, 1964, Phila. Phils	8	8	8	5	2	4	35	7	4	4	5	2	4	26	61
Dick Nen, 1963, Chicago Cubs	4	6	8	6	4	5	29	6	6	6	5	3	6	32	61
Mike Epstein, 1966, Wash. Sen.	8	9	8	4	2	3	34	8	4	5	4	2	4	27	61
Gary Holman (3), 1968, Wash. Sen.	0	4	10	6	0	5	25	0	0	6	6	0	6	18	43
Ricardo Joseph (3), 1964, Phila. Ph.	0	4	8	4	0	3	19	1	3	6	6	1	5	22	41
Greg Goosen (3), 1965, N.Y. Mets	1	3	7	3	0	3	17	0	3	3	3	1	4	14	31

POSITION
SECOND BASE

	First Game in Major Leagues (or Years in Major Leagues)	Team	Offensive Total	Defensive Total	Total Rating
Bill Mazeroski	1956	Pit. Pirates	47	70	117
Dick McAuliffe	1960	Det. Tigers	51	40	91
Glenn Beckert	1965	Chicago Cubs	47	43	90
Julian Javier	1960	St. L. Cardinals	44	46	90
Tommy Helms	1964	Cin. Reds	44	45	89
Rod Carew	1967	Minn. Twins	52	37	89
Mike Andrews	1966	Boston Red Sox	41	46	87
Joe Morgan	1963	Houston Astros	46	40	86
Felix Millan	1966	Atlanta Braves	44	42	86
Bob Knoop	1964	Calif. Angels	36	47	83
Dave Johnson	1965	Balt. Orioles	38	44	82
Ron Hunt	1963	S. F. Giants	47	35	82
Cookie Rojas	1962	Phila. Phils	42	34	76
Jim Lefebvre	1965	L. A. Dodgers	43	33	76
Jerry Adair	1958	K. C. Royals	35	38	73
Horace Clarke	1965	N. Y. Yankees	35	37	72
Dick Green	1964	Oakland A's	32	40	72
John Donaldson	1966	Oakland A's	37	35	72
Ken Boswell	1967	N. Y. Mets	40	32	72
Bernie Allen	1962	Wash. Senators	31	34	65
Wayne Causey	1955	Atlanta Braves	40	25	65
Paul Popavich	1964	L. A. Dodgers	29	33	62
Dalton Jones	1964	Boston Red Sox	40	20	60
Phil Linz	1961	N. Y. Mets	28	32	60
Chuck Hiller	1961	Pit. Pirates	40	20	60
Dick Tracewski	1962	Detroit Tigers	20	38	58
Frank Quilici	1965	Minn. Twins	26	28	54
Dave Nelson (3)	1968	Cleve. Indians	28	23	51

**POSITION
SECOND BASE
(continued)**

	First Game in Major Leagues (or Years in Major Leagues)	Team	Offensive Total	Defensive Total	Total Rating
Sandy Alomar	1964	Chicago White Sox	14	33	47
Vern Fuller	1964	Cleve. Indians	20	25	45
Nate Oliver	1963	S. F. Giants	20	25	45
Chuck Cottier	1964	Calif. Angels	9	23	32
Tim Cullen	1966	Wash. Senators	9	23	32

Players with Uncharted Scores

Bob Heise (1) (A)	1967	N. Y. Mets
Bob Schoder (2)	1965	S. F. Giants
Hal McRae (2)	1968	Houston Astros
Bill Harris (2)	1968	K. C. Royals
Bart Shirley (2)	1968	L. A. Dodgers
Frank Coggins (1)	1967	Wash. Senators
Dave Campbell (1)	1967	Detroit Tigers
Ralph Garr (1)	1968	Atlanta Braves

A. Heise also performs as shortstop, and is excellent prospect in Met organization.

POSITION RATED: SECOND BASE

	OFFENSIVE CATEGORICALS							DEFENSIVE CATEGORICALS							
	1-TEAM VALUE	2-POWER	3-TECHNICAL PROFICIENCY	4-SPEED	5-EXPERIENCE	6-VERSATILITY AND EXECUTION	THE OFFENSIVE TOTALS	1-TEAM VALUE	2-POWER	3-TECHNICAL PROFICIENCY	4-SPEED	5-EXPERIENCE	6-VERSATILITY AND EXECUTION	THE DEFENSIVE TOTALS	TOTAL POINTS OF PLAYER
Rating Scale in points:	25	25	25	10	10	10	105 Max	20	10	10	10	10	10	70	175 Max (ideal)
Bill Mazeroski, 1956, Pit. Pirates	10	8	10	4	10	5	47	20	10	10	10	10	10	70	117
Dick McAuliffe, 1960, Det. Tigers	13	11	12	5	5	5	51	12	6	6	5	5	6	40	91
Glenn Beckert, 1965, Chi. Cubs	10	10	12	5	4	6	47	12	6	7	7	4	7	43	90
Julian Javier, 1960, St. L. Cards.	9	8	10	6	6	5	44	12	7	7	7	7	6	46	90
Tommy Helms, 1964, Cin Reds	9	8	11	6	4	6	44	13	7	7	7	4	7	45	89
Rod Carew, 1967, Minn. Twins	12	9	13	7	4	7	52	10	6	6	6	4	5	37	89
Mike Andrews, 1966, Bos. Red Sox	9	6	10	6	4	6	41	12	7	7	8	5	7	46	87
Joe Morgan, 1963, Houston Astros	10	9	11	6	5	5	46	10	6	6	7	5	6	40	86
Felix Millan, 1966, Atl. Braves	10	8	11	7	3	5	44	11	7	7	7	3	7	42	86
Bobby Knoop, 1964, Calif. Angels	7	8	8	4	5	4	36	12	8	8	7	5	7	47	83
Dave Johnson, 1965, Balt. Orioles	8	7	9	5	4	5	38	12	7	7	7	4	7	44	82
Ron Hunt, 1963, S.F. Giants	11	8	11	5	5	7	47	10	5	5	5	5	5	35	82
Cookie Rojas, 1962, Phila. Phils	10	7	10	4	5	6	42	9	5	5	5	5	5	34	76
Jim Lefebvre, 1965, L.A. Dodgers	9	10	10	5	4	5	43	8	5	5	5	4	6	33	76
Jerry Adair, 1958, K.C. Royals	5	6	8	5	6	5	35	5	8	8	5	6	6	38	73
Horace Clarke, 1965, N.Y. Yankees	8	5	8	5	4	5	35	10	6	6	6	4	5	37	72
Dick Green, 1964, Oakland A's	5	7	8	4	4	4	32	6	7	8	7	5	7	40	72
John Donaldson, 1966, Oakland A's	7	8	9		3	5	37	8	6	6	6	3	6	35	72

POSITION RATED: SECOND BASE (continued)

	OFFENSIVE CATEGORICALS							DEFENSIVE CATEGORICALS							
	1-TEAM VALUE	2-POWER	3-TECHNICAL PROFICIENCY	4-SPEED	5-EXPERIENCE	6-VERSATILITY AND EXECUTION	THE OFFENSIVE TOTALS	1-TEAM VALUE	2-POWER	3-TECHNICAL PROFICIENCY	4-SPEED	5-EXPERIENCE	6-VERSATILITY AND EXECUTION	THE DEFENSIVE TOTALS	TOTAL POINTS OF PLAYER
Rating Scale in points:	25	25	25	10	10	10	105 Max	20	10	10	10	10	10	70	175 Max (ideal)
Ken Boswell, 1967, N.Y. Mets	8	8	10	6	2	6	40	7	6	6	6	2	5	32	72
Bernie Allen, 1962, Wash. Senators	7	5	7	4	4	4	31	8	6	6	5	4	5	34	65
Wayne Causey, 1955, Atl. Braves	7	5	8	5	7	8	40	4	3	4	4	5	5	25	65
Paul Popovich, 1964, L.A. Dodgers	6	5	7	5	2	4	29	7	6	6	5	3	6	33	62
Chuck Hiller, 1961, Pit. Pirates	8	7	10	4	5	6	40	3	4	3	3	4	3	20	60
Dalton Jones, 1964, Bos. Red Sox	7	8	10	6	3	6	40	3	3	3	5	2	4	20	60
Phil Linz, 1961, N.Y. Mets	4	4	6	5	4	5	28	5	5	5	5	6	6	32	60
Dick Tracewski, 1962, Det. Tigers	2	2	5	4	4	3	20	8	6	6	6	5	7	38	58
Frank Quilici, 1965, Minn. Twins	4	3	6	4	4	5	26	4	5	5	5	3	6	28	54
Dave Nelson (3), 1968, Cleve. Ind.	5	2	5	8	1	7	28	1	3	5	7	1	6	23	51
Sandy Alomar, 1964, Chi. White Sox	2	0	2	6	2	2	14	5	5	6	6	4	7	33	47
Vern Fuller, 1964, Cleve. Ind.	5	2	5	4	1	3	20	2	6	6	5	1	5	25	45
Nate Oliver, 1963, S.F. Giants	2	1	5	4	4	4	20	5	4	4	4	4	4	25	45
Tim Cullen, 1966, Wash. Senators	0	1	1	4	2	1	9	0	4	5	5	4	5	23	32
Chuck Cottier, 1964, Calif. Angels	0	1	1	4	2	1	9	0	5	5	5	3	5	23	32

POSITION: SHORTSTOP

Name	First Game in Major Leagues (or Years in Major Leagues)	Team	Offensive Total	Defensive Total	Total Rating
Ernie Banks (A)	1953	Chicago Cubs	74	45	119
Maurey Wills	1959	Montreal Expos	62	49	111
Luis Aparicio	1956	Chi. White Sox	44	64	108
Jim Fregosi	1961	Calif. Angels	49	52	101
Lee Cardenas	1960	Cin. Reds	44	50	94
"Campy" Campaneris	1964	Oakland A's	45	49	94
Zoilo Versailes	1959	San Diego Padres	42	50	92
Don Kessinger	1964	Chi. Cubs	39	50	89
Gene Alley	1963	Pit. Pirates	39	47	86
Rico Petrocelli	1963	Boston Red Sox	42	41	83
Dal Maxvill	1962	St. L. Cardinals	33	49	82
Bud Harrelson	1965	N.Y. Mets	32	47	79
Sonny Jackson	1963	Atlanta Braves	32	44	76
Dennis Menke	1962	Houston Astros	41	35	76
Mark Belanger	1966	Balt. Orioles	28	47	75
Woody Held	1954	Chi. White Sox	45	30	75
Tom Tresh	1961	N.Y. Yankees	44	31	75
Ron Hansen	1958	Wash. Senators	36	35	71
Jose Pagan	1959	Pit. Pirates	36	35	71
Hal Lanier	1964	S. F. Giants	30	41	71
Larry Brown	1963	Cleve. Indians	34	34	68
Bob Johnson (B)	1960	Atl. Braves	43	25	68
Ray Oyler	1965	Seattle Pilots	20	48	68
Woody Woodward	1964	Cin. Reds	28	40	68
Dick Schofield	1953	St. L. Cardinals	35	33	68
Hector Torres	1968	Houston Astros	28	37	65
Bobby Wine	1960	Phila. Phils	24	38	62
Ruben Amaro	1958	Calif. Angels	25	37	62

POSITION
SHORTSTOP
(continued)

	First Game in Major Leagues (or Years in Major Leagues)	Team	Offensive Total	Defensive Total	Total Rating
Al Weiss	1962	N. Y. Mets	18	44	62
Ed Brinkman (C)	1961	Wash. Senators	13	44	57
Tito Fuentes (2)	1965	S. F. Giants	31	26	57
Roberto Pena (3)	1965	San Diego Padres	26	31	57
Julio Gotay	1960	Houston Astros	26	26	52
Fred Patek (3)	1968	Pit. Pirates	21	31	52
Felix Martinez	1962	Atl. Braves	22	28	50
Ted Kubiak	1967	Oakland A's	22	28	50
Ron Clark (3)	1966	Minn. Twins	17	30	47
Gary Sutherland	1966	Montreal Expos	23	24	47
Gene Michael (D)	1966	N. Y. Yankees	9	33	42
John Kennedy	1962	N. Y. Yankees	15	26	41
Jack Hernandez (3)	1967	K. C. Royals	13	28	41
Tom Matchick (3)	1967	Detroit Tigers	20	20	40
Jose Arcia (3)	1968	San Diego Padres	15	23	38
Rick Renick (3)	1968	Minn. Twins	16	22	38
Lee Elia (3)	1966	Chicago Cubs	15	23	38

A. Banks presently is playing first base. Majority of career was shortstop.

B. Johnson plays all other infield positions with equal facility.

C. Fuentes rating based on previous major league experience, through 1967 season.

D. Kennedy was in Minor leagues in 1968. Rating is based on previous major league experience.

POSITION
SHORTSTOP

	First Game in Major Leagues (or Years in Major Leagues)	Team	Offensive Total	Defensive Total	Total Rating
Players with Uncharted Scores					
Jerry Kenney (2) (A)	1967	N. Y. Yankees			
Bob Murcer (2) (B)	1965	N. Y. Yankees			
Gil Garrido (1)	1968	Atlanta Braves			
Ed Leon (1) (C)	1968	Cleve. Indians			
Don Money (1) (D)	1968	Phila. Phils			
Ceasar Gutierrez (1)	1967	S. F. Giants			
Leon McFadden (1) (E)	1968	Houston Astros			
Rich Morales (1)	1967	Chi. White Sox			
Don Mason (1)	1967	S. F. Giants			
Luis Alvarado (1)	1968	Boston Red Sox			
Angel Hermoso (1)	1967	Montreal Expos			
Jim Williams (1)	1966	Montreal Expos			

A. Kenney was in military service in 1968 season. Will be available for 1969; excellent prospect.

B. Murcer was in military service during 1968 season. Will be available for 1969; excellent prospect.

C. Leon one of best prospects in Cleveland organization.

D. Money good prospect for 1969 season.

E. McFadden also can perform at Catcher's position.

POSITION RATED: SHORTSTOP

	OFFENSIVE CATEGORICALS							DEFENSIVE CATEGORICALS							
	1-TEAM VALUE	2-POWER	3-TECHNICAL PROFICIENCY	4-SPEED	5-EXPERIENCE	6-VERSATILITY AND EXECUTION	THE OFFENSIVE TOTALS	1-TEAM VALUE	2-POWER	3-TECHNICAL PROFICIENCY	4-SPEED	5-EXPERIENCE	6-VERSATILITY AND EXECUTION	THE DEFENSIVE TOTALS	TOTAL POINTS OF PLAYER
Rating Scale in points:	25	25	25	10	10	10	105 Max	20	10	10	10	10	10	70	175 Max (ideal)
Ernie Banks, 1953, Chicago Cubs	18	19	15	6	10	6	74	12	6	6	5	10	6	45	119
Maurey Wills, 1959, Montreal Expos	16	8	9	10	9	10	62	10	7	7	8	10	7	49	111
Luis Aparico, 1956, Chi. White Sox	9	7	8	8	5	7	44	18	9	9	9	10	9	64	108
Jim Fregosi, 1961, Calif. Angels	11	10	12	6	5	5	49	14	9	8	8	5	8	52	101
Leo Cardenas, 1960, Cin. Reds	9	10	9	5	6	5	44	14	7	7	7	7	8	50	94
"Campy" Campaneris, 1964, Oak. A's	11	7	9	8	4	6	45	14	7	6	10	5	7	49	94
Zoilo Versalles, 1959, San Diego Pad	10	8	8	6	5	5	42	14	8	7	8	6	7	50	92
Don Kessinger, 1964, Chi. Cubs	9	6	9	6	4	5	39	15	8	8	8	4	7	50	89
Gene Alley, 1963, Pit. Pirates	8	8	8	5	5	5	39	12	8	8	7	5	7	47	86
Rico Petrocelli, 1963, Bos. Red Sox	9	10	10	5	4	4	42	10	8	7	6	4	6	41	83
Dal Maxvill, 1962, St. L. Cards.	6	5	7	5	5	5	33	13	8	8	7	5	8	49	82
Budd Harrelson, 1965, N.Y. Mets	7	4	7	7	3	4	32	13	8	8	8	3	7	47	79
Sonny Jackson, 1965, Atl. Braves	6	4	7	7	3	5	32	12	7	7	8	4	6	44	76
Dennis Menke, 1962, Hou. Astros	10	9	9	4	5	4	41	10	5	5	5	5	5	35	76
Mark Belanger, 1966, Balt. Orioles	5	6	6	6	2	3	28	14	8	8	8	2	7	47	75
Woody Held, 1954, Chi. White Sox	9	11	9	4	8	4	45	6	5	5	4	4	6	30	75
Tom Tresh, 1961, N.Y. Yankees	10	11	9	5	5	4	44	8	5	4	4	5	5	31	75
Ron Hansen, 1958, Wash. Senators	8	8	8	3	5	4	36	10	5	5	4	6	5	35	71
Jose Pagan, 1959, Pit. Pirates	7	8	8	4	5	4	36	10	5	5	5	5	5	35	71

POSITION RATED: SHORTSTOP (continued)

	OFFENSIVE CATEGORICALS						DEFENSIVE CATEGORICALS							
	1-TEAM VALUE	2-POWER	3-TECHNICAL PROFICIENCY	4-SPEED	5-EXPERIENCE	6-VERSATILITY AND EXECUTION	THE OFFENSIVE TOTALS	1-TEAM VALUE	2-POWER	3-TECHNICAL PROFICIENCY	4-SPEED	5-EXPERIENCE	6-VERSATILITY AND EXECUTION	THE DEFENSIVE TOTALS	TOTAL POINTS OF PLAYER
Rating Scale in points:	25	25	25	10	10	10	105 Max	20	10	10	10	10	10	70	175 Max (ideal)
Hal Lanier, 1964, S.F. Giants	6	5	6	5	4	4	30	10	6	6	7	5	7	41	71
Bob Johnson, 1960, Atl. Braves	9	9	10	5	5	5	43	5	5	6	3	3	3	25	68
Larry Brown, 1963, Cleve. Indians	7	6	7	5	4	5	34	9	5	5	5	5	5	34	68
Ray Oyler, 1965, Seattle Pilots	3	4	4	3	3	3	20	13	8	8	7	5	7	48	68
Woody Woodward, 1964, Cin. Reds	4	4	7	5	3	5	28	11	6	6	6	5	6	40	68
Dick Schofield, 1953, St. L. Cards	6	4	8	5	6	6	35	7	5	5	5	6	5	33	68
Hector Torres, 1968, Hou. Astros	7	4	7	5	1	4	28	11	6	7	7	1	5	37	65
Bobby Wine, 1960, Phila. Phils	4	5	6	3	3	3	24	9	7	6	5	5	6	38	62
Ruben Amaro, 1958, Calif. Angels	5	1	5	5	5	4	25	10	5	6	5	5	6	37	62
Al Weis, 1962, N.Y. Mets	3	0	4	5	3	3	18	11	7	7	7	5	7	44	62
Ed Brinkman, 1961, Wash. Senators	0	0	3	4	4	2	13	11	7	7	7	5	7	44	57
Roberto Pena, 1965, San Diego Pad.	4	3	6	6	2	5	26	8	5	5	5	3	5	31	57
Julio Gotay, 1960, Hou. Astros	3	2	7	5	2	5	26	6	4	4	4	4	4	26	52
Fred Patek (3), 1968, Pit. Pirates	0	2	7	7	0	5	21	4	6	6	7	2	6	31	52
Felix Martinez, 1962, Atl. Braves	3	2	6	5	3	3	22	8	4	4	4	4	4	28	50
Ted Kubiak, 1967, Oakland A's	1	4	7	5	2	3	22	2	6	6	6	2	6	28	50
Ron Clark (3), 1966, Minn. Twins	3	1	6	4	0	3	17	5	6	6	6	1	6	30	47
Gary Sutherland, 1966, Mon. Expos	3	2	6	5	3	4	23	2	5	5	5	2	5	24	47

POSITION RATED: SHORTSTOP (continued)

	OFFENSIVE CATEGORICALS							DEFENSIVE CATEGORICALS							
	1-TEAM VALUE	2-POWER	3-TECHNICAL PROFICIENCY	4-SPEED	5-EXPERIENCE	6-VERSATILITY AND EXECUTION	THE OFFENSIVE TOTALS	1-TEAM VALUE	2-POWER	3-TECHNICAL PROFICIENCY	4-SPEED	5-EXPERIENCE	6-VERSATILITY AND EXECUTION	THE DEFENSIVE TOTALS	TOTAL POINTS OF PLAYER
Rating Scale in points:	25	25	25	10	10	10	105 Max	20	10	10	10	10	10	70	175 Max (ideal)
Gene Michael, 1966, N.Y. Yankees	0	0	1	4	2	2	9	9	5	5	5	4	5	33	42
Jack Hernandez (3), 1967, K.C. Roy.	1	2	3	3	1	3	13	2	6	6	7	2	5	28	41
Tom Matchick (3), 1967, Det. Tigers	2	1	7	5	1	4	20	4	3	5	5	1	4	20	40
Jose Arcia (3), 1968, San Diego Pad.	1	0	5	5	1	3	15	2	5	5	5	1	5	23	38
Rick Rennick (3), 1968, Minn. Twins	1	1	7	4	1	2	16	1	5	5	5	1	5	22	38
Lee Elia (3), 1966, Chicago Cubs	1	1	6	4	0	3	15	2	4	5	5	2	5	23	38

**POSITION
THIRD BASE**

	First Game in Major Leagues (or Years in Major Leagues)	Team	Offensive Total	Defensive Total	Total Rating
Brooks Robinson	1955	Balt. Orioles	58	70	128
Ron Santo	1960	Chicago Cubs	61	57	118
Ken Boyer	1955	L. A. Dodgers	60	58	118
Richie Allen	1963	Phila. Phils	75	29	104
Tony Perez	1964	Cin. Reds	59	43	102
Clete Boyer	1955	Atlanta Braves	39	63	102
Don Wert	1963	Detroit Tigers	39	53	102
Jim Davenport	1958	S. F. Giants	38	54	92
Jim Ray Hart	1963	S. F. Giants	62	30	92
Max Alvis	1962	Cleve. Indians	43	38	81
Deron Johnson	1960	Atlanta Braves	47	34	81
Make Shannon	1962	St. L. Cardinals	48	33	81
Joey Foy	1966	K. C. Royals	41	39	80
Bob Aspromonte	1956	Houston Astros	39	39	78
Ken McMullin	1962	Wash. Senators	39	39	78
Ed Charles	1962	N. Y. Mets	44	34	78
Don Buford	1963	Balt. Orioles	48	30	78
Ceasar Tovar	1965	Minn. Twins	44	33	77
Sal Bando	1966	Oakland A's	40	36	76
Tony Taylor	1958	Phila. Phils	35	38	73
Pete Ward	1961	Chi. White Sox	47	26	73
Doug Rader (3)	1967	Houston Astros	38	35	73
Bob Bailey	1962	Montreal Expos	38	31	69
Paul Schaal	1964	K. C. Royals	31	34	65
Chico Salmon	1964	Seattle Pilots	33	30	63
Kevin Collins (3)	1965	N. Y. Mets	27	36	63
Rich Rollins	1961	Seattle Pilots	33	30	63
Aurelio Rodriguez (3)	1967	Calif. Angels	30	33	63

POSITION
THIRD BASE
(continued)

	First Game in Major Leagues (or Years in Major Leagues)	Team	Offensive Total	Defensive Total	Total Rating
Frank Johnson (3)	1966	S. F. Giants	30	30	60
Charley Smith	1960	N. Y. Yankees	31	29	60
Chico Ruiz	1964	Cin. Reds	22	35	57
Jerry Buchek	1961	N. Y. Mets	28	28	56
Ed Spiezio	1964	St. L. Cardinals	27	26	53
Bobby Cox	1968	N. Y. Yankees	25	28	53
Phil Gagliano	1963	St. L. Cardinals	26	26	52
Jose Herrera (3) (A)	1968	Montreal Expos	24	22	46
Dick Kenworthy	1962	Chicago White Sox	18	22	40

A. Herrera also can play outfield positions.

Players with Uncharted Scores

Mike Ferraro (2)	1966	Seattle Pilots
Winston Llenas (1)	1968	Calif. Angels
Bill Sudakis (2) (A)	1968	L. A. Dodgers
Joe Moock (1) (B)	1967	N. Y. Mets
Bob Etheridge (1) (C)	1967	S. F. Giants
Bill Melton (1)	1967	Chicago White Sox
Rich Billings (1) **(CD)**	1968	Wash. Senators

A. Sudakis excellent prospect for 1969 season.

B. Moock prospects limited for 1969 season.

C. Etheridge prospects fair for 1969 season.

D. Also can play outfield.

POSITION RATED: THIRD BASE

	OFFENSIVE CATEGORICALS							DEFENSIVE CATEGORICALS							
	1-TEAM VALUE	2-POWER	3-TECHNICAL PROFICIENCY	4-SPEED	5-EXPERIENCE	6-VERSATILITY AND EXECUTION	THE OFFENSIVE TOTALS	1-TEAM VALUE	2-POWER	3-TECHNICAL PROFICIENCY	4-SPEED	5-EXPERIENCE	6-VERSATILITY AND EXECUTION	THE DEFENSIVE TOTALS	TOTAL POINTS OF PLAYER
Rating Scale in points:	25	25	25	10	10	10	105 Max	20	10	10	10	10	10	70	175 Max (ideal)
Brooks Robinson, 1955, Balt. Orioles	13	12	13	5	10	5	58	20	10	10	10	10	10	70	128
Ron Santo, 1960, Chi. Cubs	16	14	14	5	7	5	61	17	8	8	8	8	8	57	118
Ken Boyer, 1955, L.A. Dodgers	13	14	13	5	10	5	60	16	8	8	8	10	8	58	118
Richie Allen, 1963, Phila. Phils	20	19	19	6	5	6	75	8	4	4	5	4	4	29	104
Tony Perez, 1964, Cin. Reds	14	14	13	7	5	6	59	12	7	7	6	5	6	43	102
Clete Boyer, 1955, Atl. Braves	8	9	8	4	6	4	39	18	9	9	8	10	9	63	102
Don Wert, 1963, Det. Tigers	8	8	9	5	4	5	39	16	8	8	8	5	8	53	92
Jim Davenport, 1958, S.F. Giants	7	8	8	4	6	5	38	14	8	8	6	10	8	54	92
Jim Ray Hart, 1963, S.F. Giants	16	16	15	5	5	5	62	8	5	4	4	5	4	30	92
Max Alvis, 1962, Cleve. Indians	10	10	9	4	5	5	43	10	6	6	5	6	5	38	81
Deron Johnson, 1960, Atl. Braves	12	12	11	4	5	3	47	10	5	5	4	5	5	34	81
Mike Shannon, 1962, St. L. Cards	12	12	12	4	4	4	48	9	5	5	5	4	5	33	81
Joey Foy, 1966, K.C. Royals	8	9	9	7	4	4	41	10	6	7	6	4	6	39	80
Bob Aspromonte, 1956, Hou. Astros	8	7	9	4	6	5	39	11	6	6	5	6	5	39	78
Ken McMullin, 1962, Wash. Senators	8	9	9	5	4	4	39	10	6	6	6	5	6	39	78
Ed Charles, 1962, N.Y. Mets	9	9	9	5	7	5	44	9	5	5	5	5	5	34	78
Don Buford, 1963, Balt. Orioles	10	10	10	7	5	6	48	5	5	5	5	4	6	30	78
Ceasar Tovar, 1965, Minn. Twins	10	8	10	6	4	6	44	8	5	5	5	4	6	33	77

POSITION RATED: THIRD BASE (continued)

	OFFENSIVE CATEGORICALS							DEFENSIVE CATEGORICALS							
	1-TEAM VALUE	2-POWER	3-TECHNICAL PROFICIENCY	4-SPEED	5-EXPERIENCE	6-VERSATILITY AND EXECUTION	THE OFFENSIVE TOTALS	1-TEAM VALUE	2-POWER	3-TECHNICAL PROFICIENCY	4-SPEED	5-EXPERIENCE	6-VERSATILITY AND EXECUTION	THE DEFENSIVE TOTALS	TOTAL POINTS OF PLAYER
Rating Scale in points:	25	25	25	10	10	10	105 Max	20	10	10	10	10	10	70	175 Max (ideal)
Sal Bando, 1966, Oakland A's	9	9	11	5	2	4	40	10	5	8	6	2	5	36	76
Tony Taylor, 1958, Phila. Phils	6	6	7	5	5	6	35	8	6	6	6	5	7	38	73
Pete Ward, 1961, Chi. White Sox	12	11	11	4	5	4	47	8	4	4	3	4	3	26	73
Doug Radar, 1967, Hou. Astros	8	8	10	5	2	5	38	10	6	6	5	2	6	35	73
Bob Bailey, 1963, Montreal Expos	8	8	8	5	4	5	38	8	5	5	5	3	5	31	69
Paul Schaal, 1964, K.C. Royals	6	7	7	5	2	4	31	8	6	6	6	2	6	34	65
Chico Salmon, 1964, Seattle Pilots	6	5	7	6	4	5	33	7	4	4	5	4	6	30	63
Kevin Collins, 1965, N.Y. Mets	4	7	7	5	1	3	27	7	7	7	7	1	7	36	63
Rich Rollins, 1961, Seattle Pilots	6	7	8	3	5	4	33	6	5	5	4	5	5	30	63
Auerio Rodriquez, 1967, Calif. Ang.	6	5	8	5	1	5	30	5	7	7	7	1	6	33	63
Frank Johnson, 1966, S.F. Giants	6	6	7	6	1	4	30	7	5	5	5	2	6	30	60
Charley Smith, 1960, N.Y. Yankees	6	8	7	3	4	3	31	5	5	5	5	4	5	29	60
Chico Ruiz, 1964, Cin. Reds	3	2	6	5	2	4	22	3	6	6	6	7	7	35	57
Jerry Buchek, 1961, N.Y. Mets	5	8	7	3	2	3	28	5	4	5	5	4	5	28	56
Ed Spiezio, 1964, St. L. Cards	2	6	7	5	3	4	27	3	5	5	4	4	5	26	53
Bobby Cox, 1968, N.Y. Yankees	6	5	6	4	1	3	25	8	4	5	5	1	5	28	53
Phil Gagliano, 1963, St. L. Cards	3	6	7	5	2	3	26	2	5	5	5	3	6	26	52
Jose Herrera (3), 1968, Mont. Exp.	0	5	8	6	0	5	24	0	5	6	6	0	5	22	46
Dick Kenworthy, 1962, Chi. White Sox	1	5	5	3	1	3	18	0	4	6	5	2	5	22	40

POSITION
LEFT FIELD

	First Game in Major Leagues (or Years in Major Leagues)	Team	Offensive Total	Defensive Total	Total Rating
Carl Yastrzemski	1961	Boston Red Sox	67	61	128
Lou Brock	1961	St. L. Cardinals	61	47	108
Willie Horton	1963	Det. Tigers	62	41	103
Billy Williams	1959	Chicago Cubs	61	41	102
Willie Stargell	1962	Pit. Pirates	58	39	97
Tommy Davis	1959	Seattle Pilots	61	32	93
Rico Carty (A)	1963	Atl. Braves	55	38	93
Rick Reichardt	1964	Calif. Angels	47	45	92
Alex Johnson	1964	Cin. Reds	55	36	91
Bob Allison	1958	Minn. Twins	46	43	89
Frank Howard	1958	Wash. Senators	55	31	86
Cleon Jones	1963	N.Y. Mets	45	39	84
Leon Wagner	1958	Chicago White Sox	53	31	84
Roy White	1965	N.Y. Yankees	42	41	83
Lou Johnson	1960	Cleve. Indians	43	40	83
Curt Blefary	1965	Balt. Orioles	42	36	78
Russ Snyder	1959	Cleve. Indians	39	37	76
Lee Maye	1959	Cleve. Indians	40	33	73
Jesus Alou	1963	Montreal Expos	38	34	72
Len Gabrielson	1960	L. A. Dodgers	38	33	71
Ty Cline	1960	Montreal Expos	32	38	70
Al Ferrara (B)	1963	San Diego Padres	35	32	67
Walt Williams	1964	Chicago White Sox	36	31	67
Curt Motton (3)	1967	Balt. Orioles	37	30	67
Fred Valentine	1959	Balt. Orioles	32	34	66
Bubba Morton	1961	Calif. Angels	32	32	64
Lennie Green	1957	Boston Red Sox	32	32	64
Mike Lum (3)	1967	Atlanta Braves	28	36	64

POSITION
LEFT FIELD
(continued)

	First Game in Major Leagues (or Years in Major Leagues)	Team	Offensive Total	Defensive Total	Total Rating
Ted Savage	1962	L. A. Dodgers	32	31	63
Tommy Aaron	1962	Atlanta Braves	32	30	62
Art Shamsky	1965	N. Y. Mets	33	24	57
Sam Bowens	1963	Wash. Senators	27	30	57
Willie Smith	1963	Chicago Cubs	27	29	56
Gates Brown	1963	Detroit Tigers	40	16	56
Hank Allen	1966	Wash. Senators	24	30	54
Jim Holt (3)	1968	Minn. Twins	28	26	54
Manny Jiminez	1962	Pit. Pirates	40	11	51
Gary Kolb	1960	Pit. Pirates	19	32	51
Frank Kostro	1962	Minn. Twins	19	30	49
Dave Marshall (3)	1967	S. F. Giants	26	22	48
Ivan Murrell (3)	1963	San Diego Padres	21	26	47
"Bull" Watson (3)	1966	Houston Astros	23	23	46
Richie Scheinblum (3)	1965	Cleve. Indians	21	23	44
Ed Kirkpatrick	1963	Calif. Angels	18	26	44
Joe Rudi (3)	1967	Oakland A's	25	19	44
Mike Page (3)	1968	Atlanta Braves	19	22	41
Tom Reymonds (2) (C)	1963	N. Y. Mets	10	21	31
Wayne Comer	1967	Seattle Pilots	18	13	31

A. Carty did not play in 1968 because of serious illness, rating based on previous major league experience.

B. Ferrara did not play in 1968 because of injury, rating through 1967.

C. Reynolds rating based on experience in majors through 1967 season.

POSITION
LEFT FIELD
(continued)

	First Game in Major Leagues (or Years in Major Leagues)	Team	Offensive Total	Defensive Total	Total Rating

Players with Uncharted Scores

Nate Colbert (2) (A)	1966	San Diego Padres			
Dave May (2)	1967	Baltimore Orioles			
Tom Shopay (1)	1967	N. Y. Yankees			
Carlos May (1)	1968	Chicago White Sox			
Bob Oliver (1) (B)	1968	K. C. Royals			

A. Colbert also can be positioned at first base.

B. Oliver has very good potential.

POSITION RATED: LEFT FIELD

	OFFENSIVE CATEGORICALS							DEFENSIVE CATEGORICALS							
	1-TEAM VALUE	2-POWER	3-TECHNICAL PROFICIENCY	4-SPEED	5-EXPERIENCE	6-VERSATILITY AND EXECUTION	THE OFFENSIVE TOTALS	1-TEAM VALUE	2-POWER	3-TECHNICAL PROFICIENCY	4-SPEED	5-EXPERIENCE	6-VERSATILITY AND EXECUTION	THE DEFENSIVE TOTALS	TOTAL POINTS OF PLAYER
Rating Scale in points:	25	25	25	10	10	10	105 Max	20	10	10	10	10	10	70	175 Max (ideal)
Carl Yastrzemski, 1961, Bos. R. S.	16	14	16	6	8	7	67	15	9	9	9	10	9	61	128
Lou Brock, 1961. St. L. Cards	15	10	13	10	6	7	61	12	7	7	8	6	7	47	108
Willie Horton, 1963, Det. Tigers	17	17	14	5	5	4	62	10	7	7	6	5	6	41	103
Billy Williams, 1959, Chi. Cubs	15	14	15	6	6	5	61	10	6	6	7	6	6	41	102
Willie Stargell, 1962, Pit. Pirates	15	16	12	4	6	5	58	10	7	7	5	5	5	39	97
Tommy Davis, 1959, Seattle Pilots	13	14	16	5	6	7	61	7	4	4	5	7	5	32	93
Rick Reichardt, 1964, Calif. Angels	11	11	10	7	4	4	47	13	7	7	7	5	6	45	92
Alex Johnson, 1964, Cin. Reds	13	12	14	6	3	7	55	10	6	6	6	3	5	36	91
Bob Allison, 1958, Minn. Twins	12	11	10	4	5	4	46	11	7	7	6	6	6	43	89
Frank Howard, 1958, Wash. Sen.	15	15	9	4	7	5	55	8	4	4	4	7	4	31	86
Cleon Jones, 1963, N.Y. Mets	10	9	10	7	4	5	45	10	6	6	7	4	6	39	84
Leon Wagner, 1958, Chi. White Sox	12	12	11	5	8	5	53	8	4	4	5	6	4	31	84
Roy White, 1965, N.Y. Yankees	9	8	9	8	3	5	42	11	6	6	7	5	6	41	83
Lou Johnson, 1960, Cleve. Indians	12	8	8	5	5	5	43	12	6	5	6	5	6	40	83
Curt Blefry, 1965, Balt. Orioles	10	11	9	4	5	3	42	9	6	6	5	5	5	36	78
Russ Snyder, 1959, Cleve. Indians	8	6	10	7	5	3	39	10	5	5	6	6	5	37	76
Lee Maye, 1959, Cleve. Indians	9	7	10	5	5	4	40	8	5	5	5	5	5	33	73
Jesus Alou, 1963, Mon. Expos	8	8	9	6	2	5	38	8	6	6	6	3	5	34	72

POSITION RATED: LEFT FIELD (continued)

	OFFENSIVE CATEGORICALS							DEFENSIVE CATEGORICALS							
	1-TEAM VALUE	2-POWER	3-TECHNICAL PROFICIENCY	4-SPEED	5-EXPERIENCE	6-VERSATILITY AND EXECUTION	THE OFFENSIVE TOTALS	1-TEAM VALUE	2-POWER	3-TECHNICAL PROFICIENCY	4-SPEED	5-EXPERIENCE	6-VERSATILITY AND EXECUTION	THE DEFENSIVE TOTALS	TOTAL POINTS OF PLAYER
Rating Scale in points:	25	25	25	10	10	10	105 Max	20	10	10	10	10	10	70	175 Max (ideal)
Len Gabrielson, 1960, L.A. Dodgers	9	9	8	4	4	4	38	9	5	5	4	5	5	33	71
Ty Cline, 1960, Montreal Expos	6	4	8	6	4	4	32	9	6	6	7	5	5	38	70
Al Ferrera, 1963, San Diego Padres	8	9	8	3	4	3	35	8	5	5	4	5	5	32	67
Walt Williams, 1964, Chi. White Sox	8	6	9	6	2	5	36	9	5	5	5	2	5	31	67
Curt Motton, 1967, Balt. Orioles	8	7	10	6	1	5	37	5	6	6	6	2	5	30	67
Fred Valentine, 1959, Balt. Orioles	7	7	8	5	2	3	32	9	6	6	5	3	5	34	66
Bubba Morton, 1961, Calif. Angels	7	6	8	4	3	4	32	8	5	5	5	4	5	32	64
Lennie Green, 1957, Bos. Red Sox	5	5	8	5	5	4	32	6	5	5	6	5	5	32	64
Mike Lum, 1967, Atl. Braves	5	5	8	5	1	4	28	8	7	7	7	2	5	36	64
Ted Savage, 1962, L.A. Dodgers	7	8	7	4	2	4	32	8	5	5	5	3	5	31	63
Tommy Aaron, 1962, Atl. Braves	7	7	7	4	4	3	32	7	5	4	5	4	5	30	62
Art Shamsky, 1965, N.Y. Mets	8	8	8	3	3	3	33	6	4	4	3	4	3	24	57
Sam Bowens, 1963, Wash. Senators	5	8	6	3	3	2	27	5	5	5	5	5	5	30	57
Willie Smith, 1963, Chicago Cubs	6	6	6	4	2	3	27	5	5	5	5	4	5	29	56
Gates Brown, 1963, Det. Tigers	9	9	13	3	2	4	40	1	3	3	3	3	3	16	56
Hank Allen, 1966, Wash. Senators	4	4	8	4	1	3	24	4	6	6	6	2	6	30	54
Jim Holt (3), 1968, Minn. Twins	4	5	10	4	1	4	28	4	5	5	5	2	5	26	54
Manny Jiminez, 1962, Pit. Pirates	9	9	12	2	4	4	40	1	2	2	2	2	2	11	51

POSITION RATED: LEFT FIELD (continued)

	OFFENSIVE CATEGORICALS						DEFENSIVE CATEGORICALS							
	1-TEAM VALUE	2-POWER	3-TECHNICAL PROFICIENCY	4-SPEED	5-EXPERIENCE	6-VERSATILITY AND EXECUTION	THE OFFENSIVE TOTALS	1-TEAM VALUE	2-POWER	3-TECHNICAL PROFICIENCY	4-SPEED	5-EXPERIENCE	6-VERSATILITY AND EXECUTION	THE DEFENSIVE TOTALS	TOTAL POINTS OF PLAYER
Rating Scale in points:	25	25	25	10	10	10	105 Max	20	10	10	10	10	10	70	175 Max (ideal)
Gary Kolb, 1960, Pit. Pirates	2	2	5	5	3	2	19	8	5	5	5	4	5	32	51
Frank Kostro, 1962, Minn. Twins	4	3	4	4	2	2	19	5	5	5	5	5	5	30	49
Dave Marshall (3), 1967, S. F. Giants	3	4	9	5	1	4	26	1	5	5	5	1	5	22	48
Ivan Murrell (3), 1963, San Diego P.	2	2	8	5	1	3	21	2	6	6	6	1	5	26	47
"Bull" Watson (3), 1966, Hou. Astros	2	5	8	4	1	3	23	2	5	5	5	1	5	23	46
Richie Scheinblum (3), 1965, Cl. Ind.	0	1	7	6	1	6	21	0	6	6	6	0	5	23	44
Ed Kirkpatrick, 1962, Calif. Angels	2	0	7	4	2	3	18	3	5	5	5	3	5	26	44
Joe Rudi, 1967, Oakland A's	4	4	9	4	1	3	25	4	2	4	5	1	3	19	44
Mike Page (3), 1968, Atl. Braves	2	0	8	5	1	3	19	1	5	5	5	1	5	22	41

POSITION
CENTERFIELD

	First Game in Major Leagues (or Years in Major Leagues)	Team	Offensive Total	Defensive Total	Total Rating
Willie Mays	1951	S. F. Giants	91	70	161
Mickey Mantle	1951	N. Y. Yankees	92	56	148
Curt Flood	1956	St. L. Cardinals	61	64	125
Vada Pinson	1959	St. L Cardinals	63	54	117
Matty Alou	1960	Pit. Pirates	61	47	108
Felipe Alou	1958	Atlanta Braves	58	49	107
Jimmy Wynn	1963	Houston Astros	55	42	97
Rick Monday	1966	Oakland A's	49	47	96
Willie Davis	1960	L. A. Dodgers	47	49	96
Tony Gonzalez	1960	San Diego Padres	54	40	94
Reggie Smith	1967	Boston Red Sox	46	45	91
Jose Cardenal	1963	Cleve. Indians	43	48	91
Paul Blair	1964	Balt. Orioles	45	43	88
Tommy Agee	1962	N. Y. Mets	35	52	87
Ted Uhlaender	1965	Minn. Twins	43	42	85
Mack Jones	1961	Montreal Expos	43	39	82
Ken Berry	1962	Chicago White Sox	38	44	82
Adolpho Phillips	1964	Chicago Cubs	37	44	81
Jimmy Hall	1963	Cleve. Indians	43	38	81
Manny Mota	1962	Montreal Expos	40	40	80
Mickey Stanley	1964	Detroit Tigers	32	48	80
Vic Davillio	1963	Calif. Angels	37	42	79
Roger Repoz	1964	Calif. Angels	38	41	79
Bobby Bonds (3) (A)	1968	S. F. Giants	40	35	75
Del Unser	1968	Wash. Senators	35	39	74
Jim Gosger	1963	Seattle Pilots	30	36	66
Don Lock	1962	Phila. Phils	31	34	65
Ron Davis	1962	St. L. Cardinals	28	37	65

POSITION
CENTERFIELD (continued)

	First Game in Major Leagues (or Years in Major Leagues)	Team	Offensive Total	Defensive Total	Total Rating
Jose Tartabull	1962	Boston Red Sox	30	35	65
Bill Robinson	1966	N.Y. Yankees	31	34	65
Buddy Bradford (3)	1966	Chicago White Sox	24	37	61
Willie Crawford (3)	1964	L. A. Dodgers	24	31	55
Don Bosch	1966	Montreal Expos	16	33	49

A. Bond's potential exceptional, if he did not accrue official rookie status in 1968 will be highly regarded for 1969 "Rookie of Year" awards.

Players with Uncharted Scores

Amos Otis (1)	1967	N.Y. Mets
Jim Beauchamp (2)	1963	Cin. Reds
Ken Henderson (1)	1965	S. F. Giants
Jose Vidal (2)	1966	Cleve. Indians
Merv Rettenmund (2) (A)	1968	Balt. Orioles
Lou Piniella (1)	1968	Seattle Pilots
Jarvis Tatum (1)	1968	Calif. Angels
Harold "Pat" Kelly (1)	1967	K. C. Royals

A. Rettenmund exceptional prospect out of Baltimore organization.

POSITION RATED: CENTERFIELD

	OFFENSIVE CATEGORICALS							DEFENSIVE CATEGORICALS							
	1-TEAM VALUE	2-POWER	3-TECHNICAL PROFICIENCY	4-SPEED	5-EXPERIENCE	6-VERSATILITY AND EXECUTION	THE OFFENSIVE TOTALS	1-TEAM VALUE	2-POWER	3-TECHNICAL PROFICIENCY	4-SPEED	5-EXPERIENCE	6-VERSATILITY AND EXECUTION	THE DEFENSIVE TOTALS	TOTAL POINTS OF PLAYER
Rating Scale in points:	25	25	25	10	10	10	105 Max	20	10	10	10	10	10	70	175 Max (ideal)
Willie Mays, 1951, S. F. Giants	23	23	19	8	10	8	91	20	10	10	10	10	10	70	161
Mickey Mantle, 1951, N. Y. Yankees	23	23	19	10	10	7	92	15	7	7	10	10	7	56	148
Curt Flood, 1956, S. L. Cards	14	10	14	6	10	7	61	18	9	9	9	10	9	64	125
Vada Pinson, 1959, St. L. Cards	14	13	13	7	10	6	63	15	7	7	8	10	7	54	117
Matty Alou, 1960, Pit. Pirates	14	8	14	10	5	10	61	13	7	7	8	5	7	47	108
Felipe Alou, 1958, Atl. Braves	13	10	12	7	10	6	58	13	7	7	8	7	7	49	107
Jimmy Wynn, 1963, Hou. Astros	14	15	11	6	5	4	55	10	7	7	8	5	5	42	97
Rick Monday, 1966, Oakland A's	12	10	11	9	2	5	49	13	7	7	10	3	7	47	96
Willie Davis, 1960, L. A. Dodgers	9	7	9	10	8	4	47	12	7	7	10	7	6	49	96
Tony Gonzalez, 1960, San Diego P.	12	12	12	6	7	5	54	10	6	6	7	6	5	40	94
Reggie Smith, 1967, Bos. Red Sox	11	10	11	7	2	5	46	13	8	8	8	3	5	45	91
Jose Cardenal, 1963, Cleve. Indians	9	8	9	8	4	5	43	15	8	8	8	4	5	48	91
Paul Blair, 1964, Balt. Orioles	10	10	11	5	4	5	45	12	7	7	7	5	5	43	88
Tommy Agee, 1962, N. Y. Mets	6	8	6	8	4	3	35	14	8	8	8	6	8	52	87
Ted Uhleander, 1965, Minn. Twins	9	8	10	7	3	6	43	12	7	7	8	3	5	42	85
Mack Jones, 1961, Mont. Expos	9	12	9	5	5	3	43	9	6	6	7	5	6	39	82
Ken Berry, 1962, Chi. White Sox	8	7	9	5	4	5	38	13	7	7	7	4	6	44	82
Adopho Phillips, 1964, Chi. Cubs	7	10	8	7	2	3	37	11	6	7	9	3	8	44	81

POSITION RATED: CENTERFIELD (continued)

	OFFENSIVE CATEGORICALS							DEFENSIVE CATEGORICALS							
	1-TEAM VALUE	2-POWER	3-TECHNICAL PROFICIENCY	4-SPEED	5-EXPERIENCE	6-VERSATILITY AND EXECUTION	THE OFFENSIVE TOTALS	1-TEAM VALUE	2-POWER	3-TECHNICAL PROFICIENCY	4-SPEED	5-EXPERIENCE	6-VERSATILITY AND EXECUTION	THE DEFENSIVE TOTALS	TOTAL POINTS OF PLAYER
Rating Scale in points:	25	25	25	10	10	10	105 Max	20	10	10	10	10	10	70	175 Max (ideal)
Jimmy Hall, 1963, Cleve. Indians	9	10	9	6	5	4	43	8	6	6	7	5	6	38	81
Manny Mota, 1962, Mont. Expos	6	8	10	6	4	6	40	9	6	7	7	5	6	40	80
Mickey Stanley, 1964, Det. Tigers	6	6	8	4	4	4	32	13	8	8	8	4	7	48	80
Vic Davillio, 1963, Calif. Angels	8	6	6	8	4	5	37	10	7	6	8	5	6	42	79
Roger Repoz, 1964, Calif. Angels	8	9	8	6	4	3	38	9	7	7	7	5	6	41	79
Booby Bonds (3), 1968, S. F. Giants	5	5	15	9	1	5	40	2	8	8	8	1	8	35	75
Del Unser (3), 1968, Wash. Sen.	8	4	8	7	2	6	35	11	7	7	7	2	5	39	74
Jim Gosger, 1963, Seattle Pilots	4	4	6	9	4	3	30	9	5	5	6	5	6	36	66
Don Lock, 1962, Phila. Phils	5	8	8	3	4	3	31	7	6	6	5	5	5	34	65
Ron Davis, 1962, St. L. Cards	5	5	7	5	2	4	28	5	8	8	8	3	5	37	65
Jose Tartabull, 1962, Bos. Red Sox	4	3	5	8	5	5	30	5	6	6	8	5	5	35	65
Bill Robinson, 1966, N. Y. Yankees	8	7	7	5	2	2	31	8	6	7	6	2	5	34	65
Buddy Bradford (3), 1966, Chi. W.S.	5	3	6	7	1	2	24	5	6	9	9	1	7	37	61
Willie Crawford (3), 1964, L. A. Dod.	0	3	10	3	0	3	24	0	8	8	8	1	6	31	55
Don Bosch, 1966, N. Y. Mets	1	2	4	6	2	1	16	3	6	8	7	3	6	33	49

POSITION
RIGHT FIELD

Name	First Game in Major Leagues (or Years in Major Leagues)	Team	Offensive Total	Defensive Total	Total Rating
Henry Aaron	1954	Atlanta Braves	88	62	150
Roberto Clemente	1955	Pit. Pirates	71	64	135
Al Kaline	1953	Detroit Tigers	68	64	132
Frank Robinson	1956	Balt. Orioles	76	53	129
Tony Oliva	1962	Minn. Twins	68	53	121
Tony Conigliaro (A)	1964	Boston Red Sox	68	53	121
Pete Rose	1963	Cin. Reds	72	41	113
Rocky Colavito	1955	N.Y. Yankees	58	53	111
John Callison	1958	Phila. Phils	49	56	105
Reggie Jackson	1967	Oakland A's	54	45	99
Ken Harrelson	1963	Boston Red Sox	57	36	93
Jim Northrup	1964	Detroit Tigers	49	44	93
Tommy Harper	1962	Seattle Pilots	37	49	86
Ron Fairly	1958	L. A. Dodgers	46	33	79
Ron Swoboda	1965	N.Y. Mets	40	39	79
Chuck Hinton	1961	Calif. Angels	41	38	79
Bobby Tolan	1965	Cin. Reds	37	39	76
Floyd Robinson (B)	1960	Free Agent	46	29	75
Larry Stahl	1964	San Diego Padres	35	39	74
Mike Hershberger	1961	Oakland A's	29	45	74
Andy Kosco	1965	N.Y. Yankees	38	35	73
Norm Miller	1965	Houston Astros	35	33	68
Brandt Alyea (3) (C)	1968	Wash. Senators	39	29	68
Cap Peterson	1962	Wash. Senators	35	32	67
Ollie Brown	1965	San Diego Padres	29	38	67
Jim Hickman	1962	Chicago Cubs	30	33	63
Ed Stroud	1966	Wash. Senators	27	36	63
Dick Simpson	1962	Houston Astros	26	36	62

POSITION
RIGHT FIELD
(continued)

	First Game in Major Leagues (or Years in Major Leagues)	Team	Offensive Total	Defensive Total	Total Rating
Doug Clemens (D)	1960	Phila. Phils	27	35	62
Al Spangler	1959	Chicago Cubs	28	34	62
Steve Whitaker (3)	1966	K. C. Royals	26	28	54
George Thomas (E)	1960	Boston Red Sox	20	33	53
Ron Fairey (3)	1968	Montreal Expos	17	29	46
Bill Voss (3)	1965	Chicago White Sox	18	29	46
Joe Keough (3)	1968	K. C. Royals	17	27	44
Allen Lewis (3)	1967	Oakland A's	16	16	32

A. Tony Conigliaro totals based on career through 1967 season. Inactive in 1968 and not charted.

B. Floyd Robinson rating based on career through 1967. In 1968 he played during last half of season intermittently with Boston Red Sox. (At time of publication, Robinson was a free agent, and could negotiate with all major league teams).

C. Alyea excellent potential for 1969. Could be rookie of year if he did not accrue the official status of rookie during 1968 season.

D. Clemens played in major leagues in previous seasons and did not play until September of 1968. Therefore rating is based on career through 1967 season.

E. George Thomas rating based on career through 1967 season. He did not play during 1968 season until very end of year.

Players with Uncharted Scores

Bob "Shorty" Raudman (1)	1966	Chicago Cubs
Clarence Gaston (1) (A)	1967	San Diego Padres
Graig Nettles (1)	1967	Minn. Twins
Gene Martin (1)	1968	Wash. Senators
Al Oliver (1)	1968	Pit. Pirates

A. Nettles came up and made sensational debut with home runs in first few games. He is strong power hitter and exceptional prospect for 1969 at Minnesota. Young Graig also can perform at third base, and first base. He will be around for some time.

POSITION RATED: RIGHT FIELD

	OFFENSIVE CATEGORICALS							DEFENSIVE CATEGORICALS							TOTAL POINTS OF PLAYER
	1-TEAM VALUE	2-POWER	3-TECHNICAL PROFICIENCY	4-SPEED	5-EXPERIENCE	6-VERSATILITY AND EXECUTION	THE OFFENSIVE TOTALS	1-TEAM VALUE	2-POWER	3-TECHNICAL PROFICIENCY	4-SPEED	5-EXPERIENCE	6-VERSATILITY AND EXECUTION	THE DEFENSIVE TOTALS	
Rating Scale in points:	25	25	25	10	10	10	105 Max	20	10	10	10	10	10	70	175 Max (ideal)
Hank Aaron, 1954, Atl. Braves	21	20	21	8	10	8	88	17	9	8	9	10	9	62	150
Roberto Clemente, 1955, Pit. Pir.	16	15	15	7	10	8	71	18	9	9	9	10	9	64	135
Al Kaline, 1953, Det. Tigers	16	14	15	7	10	6	68	18	9	9	9	10	9	64	132
Frank Robinson, 1956, Balt. Orioles	18	18	17	6	10	7	76	14	7	7	7	10	8	53	129
Tony Oliva, 1962, Minn. Twins	15	14	17	7	6	9	68	15	8	8	8	6	8	53	121
Pete Rose, 1963, Cin. Reds	17	13	17	10	5	10	72	10	6	6	8	5	6	41	113
Rocky Colavito, 1955, N.Y. Yankees	12	17	11	4	10	4	58	13	8	8	7	10	7	53	111
John Callison, 1958, Phila. Phils	12	10	10	5	7	5	49	15	9	9	7	8	8	56	105
Reggie Jackson, 1967, Oakland A's	12	15	13	7	2	5	54	12	8	8	8	2	7	45	99
Ken Harrelson, 1963, Bos. Red Sox	14	14	14	6	4	5	57	8	6	6	5	5	6	36	93
Jim Northrup, 1964, Det. Tigers	11	11	11	6	4	6	49	10	8	8	8	4	6	44	93
Tommy Harper, 1962, Sea. Pilots	7	6	7	7	5	5	37	10	8	9	9	5	8	49	86
Ron Fairly, 1958, L.A. Dodgers	12	10	10	4	5	5	46	8	5	5	5	5	5	33	79
Ron Swoboda, 1965, N.Y. Mets	10	10	10	5	2	3	40	9	7	7	6	4	6	39	79
Chuck Hinton, 1961, Calif. Angels	6	9	10	7	5	4	41	10	5	5	6	6	6	38	79
Bobby Tolan, 1965, Cin. Reds	8	5	10	8	1	5	37	8	8	8	8	1	6	39	76
Larry Stahl, 1964, San Diego Padres	7	6	10	6	1	5	35	8	7	7	8	2	7	39	74
Mike Hershberger, 1961, Oak. A's	5	5	5	6	5	3	29	10	8	8	8	5	6	45	74

POSITION RATED: RIGHT FIELD (continued)

	OFFENSIVE CATEGORICALS							DEFENSIVE CATEGORICALS							
	1-TEAM VALUE	2-POWER	3-TECHNICAL PROFICIENCY	4-SPEED	5-EXPERIENCE	6-VERSATILITY AND EXECUTION	THE OFFENSIVE TOTALS	1-TEAM VALUE	2-POWER	3-TECHNICAL PROFICIENCY	4-SPEED	5-EXPERIENCE	6-VERSATILITY AND EXECUTION	THE DEFENSIVE TOTALS	TOTAL POINTS OF PLAYER
Rating Scale in points:	25	25	25	10	10	10	105 Max	20	10	10	10	10	10	70	175 Max (ideal)
Andy Kosco, 1965, N.Y. Yankees	10	10	7	3	3	3	36	8	6	6	5	5	5	35	71
Norm Miller, 1965, Hou. Astros	6	8	11	5	1	4	35	6	7	7	7	2	5	34	69
Brand't Aylea (3), 1968, Wash. Sen.	7	8	14	5	1	4	39	6	4	7	5	2	5	29	68
Cap Peterson, 1962, Wash. Senators	7	7	8	4	5	4	35	7	5	5	5	5	5	32	67
Ollie Brown, 1965, San Diego Pad.	6	8	6	4	2	3	29	7	7	8	7	4	5	38	67
Jim Hickman, 1962, Chi. Cubs	5	7	7	4	5	2	30	6	6	5	6	5	5	33	63
Ed Stroud, 1966, Wash. Senators	6	4	6	6	2	3	27	8	6	7	7	3	5	36	63
Dick Simpson, 1962, Hou. Astros	4	5	6	6	2	3	26	5	8	8	8	2	5	36	62
Al Spangler, 1959, Chi. Cubs	5	3	5	5	5	5	28	7	5	5	7	5	5	34	62
Steve Whitaker, 1966, K.C. Royals	0	8	8	6	1	3	26	9	7	7	7	2	5	28	54
Ron Fairey, 1968, Mont. Expos	3	1	5	5	0	3	17	4	6	6	7	1	5	29	46
Bill Voss, 1965, Chi. White Sox	3	2	5	5	1	2	18	3	6	6	6	1	6	28	46
Joe Keough, 1968, K.C. Royals	3	1	5	6	0	2	17	2	6	6	6	1	6	27	44
Allen Lewis, 1967, Oakland A's	0	0	1	10	0	5	16	0	0	4	7	0	5	16	32

13

Major League Aspirants

Every year youngsters enter major league training camps hoping to land a job. This year is somewhat different from the others. Because of the drafts caused by expansion, there will be many more openings, and many of the talented young minor leaguers will make the parent clubs. On the pages to follow is a sampling of such players, each without major league experience through the 1968 season.

They will be hoping to pass spring training inspection, and with the intensive drilling, examination and coaching, some of them just might be ready to make the majors. Some will have the distinction of being called "A Major League Ball Player." Of course many of them, because of inability, inexperience, and lack of opportunity will be sent to one of the minor league affiliates for further seasoning.

Some of the players to keep an eye on at this time—for they do have ability—are:

Pitchers: Bob Reynolds, Dave Roberts, Gary Timberlake, Jim Rooker, Gary Gentry, Jon Matlack, Ken Reynolds, Leon Everitt, Santiago Guzman, Harry Parker, and Mickey Scott. By the way Scott was in military service during 1968 along with Jesse Higgins of the Giants.

Catchers: Fred Kendell and Ted Sizemore have good potential.

Infielders: Dennis Doyle, Bill Grabarkewitz, Van Kelly. (Kelly and Doyle are real good prospects.)

Outfielders: Larry Hisle, LeRon Lee, Danny Walton. Both Lee and Walton are excellent prospects, with young LeRon Lee maybe the best in St. Louis's entire organization.

POSITION—PITCHER	ORGANIZATION
Gary Gentry	N.Y. Mets
Jon Matlack	N.Y. Mets
Ken Reynolds	Phila. Phils
Mike Wegner	Montreal Expos
Bob Reynolds	Montreal Expos
Jerry Robertson	Montreal Expos
Carl Morton	Montreal Expos
Ernest McAnally	Montreal Expos
John Glass	Montreal Expos
Clay Kirby	San Diego Padres
Frank Reberger	San Diego Padres
Mike Corkins	San Diego Padres
Richard James	San Diego Padres
Dave Roberts	San Diego Padres
Fred Katawczik	San Diego Padres
Steve Arlin	San Diego Padres
Charles Bates	Seattle Pilots
Dick Baney	Seattle Pilots
John Miklos	Seattle Pilots
Gary Timberlake	Seattle Pilots
Robert Richmond	Seattle Pilots

Paul Click	Seattle Pilots
Jim Rooker	Kansas City Royals
Bill Butler	Kansas City Royals
Rich Drago	Kansas City Royals
Don O'Riley	Kansas City Royals
Al Fitzmorris	Kansas City Royals
Gerald Cram	Kansas City Royals
Ed Brookens	Kansas City Royals
Mike Abarbanel	Chicago White Sox
Gary Boyd	Cleveland Indians
Joe Brauer	Detroit Tigers
Bill Burbach	N.Y. Yankees
Deano Burk	Chicago Cubs
Harold "twiggy" Clem	Phila. Phils
Larry Colton	Phila. Phils
Ron Constantino	Cleveland Indians
Mike Davison	S.F. Giants
Ricardo Delgado	Baltimore Orioles
Bob Delong	S.F. Giants
Joe Difabio	St. Louis Cardinals
Rick Evans Jr.	Calif. Angels
Leon "koot" Everitt	L.A. Dodgers
Bill Farmer	Boston Red Sox
Jim Fink	N.Y. Yankees
Ted Ford	Cleveland Indians
Ken Frailing	Chicago White Sox
Gene Garber	Pittsburgh Pirates
Vern Geishert	Calif. Angels
Bill Gogolewski	Washington Senators
Tom Griffin	Houston Astros
Santiago Guzman	St. Louis Cardinals
Rick Hense	Washington Senators
Rick Hoban Jr.	Boston Red Sox
Jesse Higgins	S.F. Giants
Dan Jaster	St. Louis Cardinals
Hal "Bucky" Jeffcoat	S.F. Giants
Ray Lamb	L.A. Dodgers
Bill Laxton	Phila. Phils
Barry Lersch	Phila. Phils
Tommy Gramly	Cleveland Indians

Tom Mandile	Chicago Cubs
Jim Moyer	S.F. Giants
Manuel Muniz	Phila. Phils
Gary Neibauer	Atlanta Braves
Moe Ogier, Jr.	Minn. Twins
Lowell Palmer	Phila. Phils
Bob Parchem	Washington Senators
Harry Parker	St. Louis Cardinals
"Big" John Parker	Phila. Phils
Bob Patrylo	Baltimore Orioles
Ron Paul	N.Y. Mets
Jerry Pruett	St. Louis Cardinals
Bob Reed	Detroit Tigers
Steve Renko	N.Y. Mets
Mickey Scott	N.Y. Yankees
Scipio Spinks	Houston Astros
Ken Tatum	Calif. Angels
Wayne Twitchell	Houston Astros
Irving Washington	Boston Red Sox
Bob Watkins	Houston Astros
Jerry Wild	Pittsburgh Pirates
Jim Wingate	Cleveland Indians
Don Yingling	Oakland Athletics
Rich Folkers	N.Y. Mets
Barry Raziano	N.Y. Mets
Gary Hill	Atlanta Braves
Don Spain	Atlanta Braves
Stan Bell	Atlanta Braves
Tom House	Atlanta Braves
Robert Wiswell	Atlanta Braves
Jim Ellis	St. Louis Cardinals

POSITION—PITCHER	ORGANIZATION
Mike Kilkeny	Detroit Tigers
Mike Small	Detroit Tigers
Jim Foor	Detroit Tigers
Norm McRae	Detroit Tigers
Dennis Saunders	Detroit Tigers
Bob Ware	Detroit Tigers

Mike Jackson   Boston Red Sox
John Thibdeau   Boston Red Sox
Fred Wenz   Boston Red Sox

POSITION—CATCHER   ORGANIZATION

Steve Chilcott   N.Y. Mets
Fred Kendell   San Diego Padres
Ron Slocum   San Diego Padres
Fran Healey   Kansas City Royals
John Ellis   N.Y. Yankees
John Sevcik   Minn. Twins (Appeared in 1965—briefly)

Ted Sizemore   L.A. Dodgers
Tom Smith   Houston Astros
Bob Didier   Atlanta Braves
Joe Cernich   Detroit Tigers

POSITION—INFIELDER   ORGANIZATION

KEY: 1—first base
     2—second base
     3—third base
     SS—shortstop
     O.F.—Outfielder also
     I.F.—Infielder

Name	Position	Organization
Gary Jestadt	S.S.	Montreal Expos
Jose Laboy	2	Montreal Expos
Frank Davanon	3-1	Montreal Expos
Rafael Robles	S.S.	San Diego Padres
Bill Haynes	2-3-S.S.	Kansas City Royals
Skippy Lockwood	2	Seattle Pilots
Udell Chambers	S.S.	Atlanta Braves
Darrel Chaney	S.S.	Cinn. Reds
Joe Cruz	1-O.F.	St. Louis Cardinals
Terry Crowley	1-O.F.	Baltimore Orioles
James DeNeff	3	Calif. Angels
Dennis Doyle	2	Phila. Phils
Bill Grabarkewitz	S.S.	L.A. Dodgers
Bill Hahn	1	Minn. Twins
Ron Hart	S.S.	Cleveland Indians

Cleo James	2-S.S. 3-O.F.	L.A. Dodgers
Van Kelly	2-S.S.	Atlanta Braves
Pete Koegel	1-O.F.	Oakland Athletics
Dick Littleton	S.S.-2	Chicago White Sox
Tim Marting	S.S.	Detroit Tigers
Bill McNulty	3	Oakland Athletics
Syd O'Brien	2-3	Boston Red Sox
Ed Pacheco	S.S.	Atlanta Braves
Gary Sprague	2	Cleveland Indians
Tommy Martinez	S.S.	N.Y. Mets
Frank Baker	I.F.	N.Y. Yankees
Gary Washington	1	N.Y. Yankees
Mike Tupedino	1	N.Y. Yankees
Len Boehmer	I.F.	N.Y. Yankees
Emerito "Jr." Lopez	S.S.	Detroit Tigers

POSITION—OUTFIELDER ORGANIZATION

Jerry Morales	San Diego Padres
James Williams	San Diego Padres
Scott Northey	Kansas City Royals
Steve Hovley	Seattle Pilots
Ted Ford	Cleveland Indians
Tom Grieve	Washington Senators
Rick Hense	Washington Senators
Larry Hisle	Phila. Phils
Leron Lee	St. Louis Cardinals
Joe Pactwa	N.Y. Yankees
Tom Simon	Chicago Cubs
Danny Walton	Houston Astros
Floyd Wicker	St. Louis Cardinals
Bernie Williams	S.F. Giants
Stan Wojcik	Oakland Athletics
Tommie Campbell	N.Y. Mets
Rod Gaspar	N.Y. Mets
Ken Singleton	N.Y. Mets
Leroy Stanton	N.Y. Mets
Ron Woods	Detroit Tigers

14

Six Categorical Rating System's All Star Teams of Players Participating in 1969 Season

The players have been selected on their career performance at their primary position. Therefore Banks and Mantle are at Shortstop and Centerfield respectively, though now in the twilight years they are playing first base.

FIRST TEAM

Position	Player	Team	Total Points
Pitcher # 1	Juan Marichal	S.F. Giants	95
Pitcher # 2	Bob Gibson	St.L. Cardinals	93

Position	Player	Team	Total Points
Catcher	Tim McCarver	St.L. Cardinals	109
First Base	Orlando Cepeda	St.L. Cardinals	122
Second Base	Bill Mazeroski	Pit. Pirates	117
Third Base	Brooks Robinson	Balt. Orioles	128
Short Stop	Ernie Banks	Chi. Cubs	119
Left Field	Carl Yastrzemski	Boston Red Sox	128
Center Field	Willie Mays	S.F. Giants	161
Right Field	Henry Aaron	Atl. Braves	150

SECOND TEAM

Position	Player	Team	Total Points
Pitcher # 1	Don Drysdale	L.A. Dodgers	86
Pitcher # 2	a. Dennis McLain	Detroit Tigers	75
Catcher	Bill Freehan	Detroit Tigers	105
First Base	Willie McCovey	S.F. Giants	105
Second Base	Dick McAuliffe	Detroit Tigers	91
Third Base	Ron Santo	Chicago Cubs	118
Short Stop	b. Maurey Wills	Montreal Expos	111
Left Field	Lou Brock	St.L. Cardinals	108
Center Field	Mickey Mantle	N.Y. Yankees	148
Right Field	Roberto Clemente	Pit. Pirates	135

a. Jim Bunning received career total of 76 points. In 1968 was with Pittsburgh. There is a strong possibility this great veteran star will retire before the 1969 season.

b. Wills played for the L. A. Dodgers at shortstop position for the majority of his career.

THIRD TEAM

Position	Player	Team	Total Points
Pitcher # 1	Mel Stottlemyre	N.Y. Yankees	74
Pitcher # 2	Dean Chance	Minnesota Twins	70
Pitcher # 3	Luis Tiant	Cleveland Indians	70
Catcher	Johnny Bench	Cincinnati Reds	104
First Base	Harmon Killebrew	Minnesota Twins	104

Second Base	Glenn Beckert	Chicago Cubs	90
	Julian Javier	St. Louis Cardinals	90
Third Base	a. Richie Allen	Philadelphia Phils	104
Short Stop	Luis Aparicio	Chicago White Sox	108
Left Field	Willie Horton	Detroit Tigers	103
Center Field	Curt Flood	St. Louis Cardinals	125
Right Field	Al Kaline	Detroit Tigers	132

a. Ken Boyer received total rating of 118 points at Third base, but at the time of this printing it was still indefinite as to his participation and availability for 1969 season. He is listed on L. A. Dodgers roster at this time.

15

The Rating System's Selections of One Year Players: the All Star Team

Points

Pitcher #1	Jerry Koosman	N.Y. Mets	54
Pitcher #2	Stan Bahnsen	N.Y. Yankees	48
Catcher	a. Johnny Bench	Cincinnati Reds	104
First Base	Gary Holman	Wash. Senators	43
Second Base	Felix Millan	Atlanta Braves	86
Third Base	Sal Bando	Oakland A's	76
Short Stop	Hector Torres	Houston Astros	65
Left Field	b. Brandt Alyea	Wash. Senators	68
Center Field	Bobby Bonds	S.F. Giants	75
Right Field	c. Reggie Jackson	Oak. Athletics	99

The One Year Pitchers of the Rating System

  Jerry Koosman: 54 points
  Stan Bahnsen: 48 points

The One Year Players of 1968 Season by Rating System Analysis

  Johnny Bench: 104 points
  Reggie Jackson: 99 points

a. Bench played 26 games in 1967 season.
b. Alyea will probably still have official rookie status in 1969.
c. Jackson played in 35 games during 1967 season.

16

The Rating System's Top Twenty Young Major Leaguers

Through the rating system we have at this time selected the young players in the game who seem to have the most potential for stardom. We have rated all of these players by the categoricals and their composites are on the charts and the comprehensive lists for their particular positions. These are the players who have achieved the highest total ratings for one year players and two year players, and none of them has of yet played three years in the "bigs."

Of all the young players in the game the following twenty, (ten pitchers and ten players) have the highest professional potential. Here are a few reasons why they can become stars or maybe super stars.

THE TOP FIVE PITCHERS GOING INTO THEIR 3RD MAJOR LEAGUE SEASON

1. TOM SEAVER, N.Y. METS.

   Has already achieved a rating of 63 points. In his first season with the lowly Mets he won 16 games, and in 1968 he convinced everyone it wasn't luck. Tom improved his E.R.A. in '68 to where it was one of the five best in the national league. This young man has "pitching class" and the ability to become one of the top pitchers in the majors for the next dozen years. Right now he is one of the best. If the Mets are to win a pennant it will be Seaver in his prime to lead them.

2. TOM PHOEBUS, BALTIMORE ORIOLES

   A rating of 55 points. In his first full year Tom won 14 games. In 1968 he improved on that and seems to be headed to that pitching ultimate, the 20 win circle, at this time. He has probably the biggest curve in the game today.

3. JIM HARDIN, BALTIMORE ORIOLES

   His rating is just under his teammate Phoebus's. Total score is 52. In 1967 he came up in the middle of the year and with his control and good fastball went on to win eight games whle losing only three. Next year he more than doubled his victories and now going into his third year seems on the threshold of stardom.

4. GARY NOLAN, CINCINNATI REDS

   Rating of 52. In 1967 at the age of 19 Gary won 14 games and had an earned run average of 2.52. In 1968 he hurt his arm and missed almost the entire season. He still won close to 10 games using mainly a great big curve and that infallible control that made him something of a marvel at the age of 19. If his arm is all right he has a chance to be the best young right-hander in baseball.

5. DON WILSON, HOUSTON ASTROS

   His chart total rating is an impressive 49. Young Don has one of the great arms in the game today, and has already pitched a no hitter, and in another game struck out 18 men. With a little more control, experience and confidence he has a chance to become a truly great pitcher.

THE TOP FIVE PITCHERS GOING INTO THEIR 2ND YEAR IN THE MAJOR LEAGUES

1. JERRY KOOSMAN, NEW YORK METS
After one year this young left hander has achieved an incredible 54 in the ratings. In his rookie year he made unbelievable pitching conquests including E.R.A. lows, and eight shutouts and complete games, and winning games—and all for that futile team the Mets put on the field. We think that he is real and expect more of the same in '69.
2. STAN BAHNSEN, NEW YORK YANKEES
A rating of 48 after one full year. The best prospect since Stottlemyre for the Yankees. This fire baller can become a great one. He has all the tools to pitch winning baseball for the rejuvenated Yankees during the next dozen years.
3. NOLAN RYAN, NEW YORK METS
This callow youth received 42 points in the ratings. This will be his second year and if blisters and the army and inexperience stay out of the way look out. He could become the best pitcher in the game this year or next, or the year after that. It is only a matter of time and putting it all together for this lad. His fast ball can be compared to the great ones, and his talent when harnessed will be as big and as exciting as any pitcher in the game—that is, in the game today or even yesterday. "The Ryan Express" is really a million dollar engine.
4. MIKE PAUL, CLEVELAND INDIANS
This young man came up to Cleveland in the middle of the year. He began throwing bullets in relief, and

didn't start much until the very end of the year. The rating is 42 at this time but the figures can shoot up as quickly as he goes to the mound. His southpaw slants have the potential to be great ones. His arm is everything the Indians could desire. Young Mike can be another of those "pitchers" that seem to go to Cleveland.

5. BOB MOOSE, PITTSBURGH PIRATES

This 21 year old right hander received a rating of 38. He only pitched about half a season in '68 and still received a good score in the categoricals. He has class, composure, control, and a good hard low pitch. It could be enough to make him a real pitching star this year.

THE TOP FIVE PLAYERS GOING INTO THEIR THIRD MAJOR LEAGUE SEASON:

1. RICK MONDAY, CENTER FIELD, OAKLAND ATHLETICS

93 points

This youngster can do it all—speed, power, defense and bat. He has already proved he can hit and field, and now will go about the business of becoming a ".300" hitter. He is quite a prospect and will be one of the best outfielders in the game for many years.

2. REGGIE SMITH, CENTER FIELD, BOSTON RED SOX

91 points

Like Rick, young Reggie can do everything well. He also will be around for some time. His arm is as good as anyone's, and his hitting should be first rate. His fielding is already exceptional.

3. ROD CAREW, SECOND BASE, MINNESOTA TWINS

89 points

His first year was 1967 and he hit .292. He also made

the all star team and was the *Sporting News* rookie of the year in the American League. In 1968 he again made the all star team and went into September battling Oliva and Yastrzemski for the batting title. This year he can go to ".300" with his bat and that could be enough to be the batting champion. He could even go higher, but we'll say ".300" in his third full season, if everything goes right.

4. LEE ANDREW MAY, FIRST BASE, CINCINNATI REDS
   87 points
   Has the power and the bat to become one of the real top hitters in the majors. In 1968 he really started producing, and now we expect a "jump" to star quality and status for Lee.
5. BOBBY TOLAN, RIGHT FIELD, CINCINNATI REDS
   76 points
   Young Bobby has been sitting while waiting to play regularly. It never happened because he was on the Cardinals and a guy named Maris was there. Of course, when the youngster did play he showed enough to grab 76 points in the ratings. This could be his year, as he might become the regular centerfielder for the Reds, they thought enough of his potential to trade the great veteran Vada Pinson for him. Bobby has speed, "tremendous speed" and will cause excitement, and create value, all the time. He might become another Lou Brock, I wonder what the Cardinal braintrust will say then?

THE TOP FIVE PLAYERS GOING INTO THEIR SECOND MAJOR LEAGUE SEASON
1. JOHN BENCH, CATCHER, CINCINNATI REDS
   104 points
   Once in awhile they come up. They look like super

stars and some of them eventually make it. Such were "Willie" and "Mickey." For a catcher John has everything and can be a super one. He is a can't miss prospect and now, going on 21, he has already had a great rookie year.

2. REGGIE JACKSON, RIGHT FIELD, OAKLAND ATHLETICS

99 points

Started hitting home runs last season with such regularity and power that he was being compared to the young Mickey Mantle of 1951. It didn't scare Reggie and we think he has the resources to become the next *great* power hitter in the majors. Another year and he might just take it all.

3. FELIX MILLAN, SECOND BASE, ATLANTA BRAVES

86 points

A real solid little ball player. He can field, hit and take charge of the infield. Will be hustling for the Braves for many more years.

4. SAL BANDO, THIRD BASE, OAKLAND ATHLETICS

76 points

The third player on the Athletics from Arizona state college. Like Monday and Jackson this second year player can be a real star. Power and glove, and did you see his arm?

5. BOBBY BONDS, CENTER FIELD, SAN FRANCISCO GIANTS

75 points

Last year he came up near the tail end of the season, but he showed more than any other center fielder in the league. If Willie is going to be moving to first base, this is the lad who can take over the pastures. His speed is comparable to Willie Davis's, and his bat could be great. Maybe another Mays, wait and see.

17

Bob Kalich Selection of the World Championship Team for 1969

In studying team strength of all the major league teams in this year of expansion one thing is quite obvious: The St. Louis Cardinals will again cause havoc in the Major Leagues. They will retain the great nucleus of starting ball players and starting pitchers from the great 1967 and 1968 teams. Furthermore they have improved themselves with trades already announced. The acquisition of the great Cincinnati center fielder Vada Pinson who will be playing right field, since Roger Maris has now retired, will give St. Louis added strength. After having mediocre seasons, comeback years for Orlando Cepeda and Tim McCarver can also be expected. Steve Carlton, the 24 year old left hander, should really blossom into a star this year, and with Lou Brock, Curt Flood, and now Vada Pinson patrolling the outfield the Cardinals can only be better. These three outfielders will be the best any club can list in the majors.

This team has all the ingredients of defense, speed, power and maturity, blended with youth and depth to become part of a great Cardinal dynasty, and we definitely feel that Bob "Hoot" Gibson will again win many of the most important games.

The team players that will give the club the most value are rated the highest collectively of any in the majors. The total score of 1134 indicates incisively the great balance of the Cardinals. On the chart to follow we have included the ratings of the players and pitchers who will be performing as starters for the St. Louis team. Compare their ratings collectively and individually to all the others, and of course to your "favorite team," and you will see why I think the St. Louis Cardinals are the club of 1969.

THE ST. LOUIS CARDINALS STARTING PLAYERS WITH THEIR RESPECTIVE INDIVIDUAL RATINGS

Pitchers:	Offensive Total:	Defensive Total:	Total Points:
Bob Gibson			93
Nelson Briles			56
Steve Carlton			55
Ray Washburn			48
RELIEF: Joe Hoerner			48
		TOTAL	300
Catcher: Tim McCarver	57	52	109
First Base: Orlando Cepeda	70	52	122
Second Base: Julian Javier	44	46	90
Shortstop: Dal Maxvill	33	49	82

Third Base: Mike Shannon	48	33	81
Left Field: Lou Brock	61	47	108
Center Field: Curt Flood	61	64	125
Right Field: Vada Pinson	63	54	117

TOTAL 834

TOTALS FOR PLAYERS AND PITCHERS: 1134

It will be predominantly with the abilities and accomplishments of these men that the Cardinals will perform and achieve in 1969. I predict that the St. Louis entry with this nucleus will win the World Championship, after winning the three of five playoff within their own league.

The 1134 total points represents the highest score of all the teams in the majors this year. Again Bob Gibson will be pitching for the Cards, and with his strong supporting cast and their confirmed abilities, as shown by the rating system's analysis, there is no doubt in my mind that they will vanquish all . . . What do you predict?

Part 2

1

Introducing the Six Categorical Rating System's All Time Major League Performers

The Encyclopedia of Baseball states that in March of 1871 The National Association of Professional Baseball Players was formed. The first National league game was played in 1876 and in 1901 the American League joined the coalition. As you know games have been played ever since. For the ratings that follow every participant who has appeared on a major league roster during season play has been considered and evaluated and charted. We have reduced the overwhelming numbers to the final total of 27 pitchers and 52 players who received the highest total scores in the rating system's analysis.

The players have been rated individually and by their

particular position on the playing field. They are only a handful of the many thousands who have played the game, but they are the standouts. Some of them have given us many thrills; some of them have given our parents and grandparents many memories, much enjoyment, and a rich perspective of how and why the game has become our heritage.

This is the 98th year of professional baseball in our country and we feel that the six categorical rating system presents the most impartial critical judgment any ball player has received to date. For the "purist" in all of us we have considered in rating the many factors that have entered and changed and influenced the game since 1871. We have thoroughly explored and evaluated and consulted all of the sources and all of the players who could be reached. We have considered the changes in parks, the change from the "dead ball" to the "live ball" to the "rabbit ball," and we have considered the factors of transportation, and schedule and hours. We feel that the ball had been changed greatly in that year of "The Babe"; and many of the men who have been consulted have said it wasn't only the ball, it was also "The Babe" who brought it to life.

We considered the differences in gloves and bat and balls, but mainly and predominantly the real changes were in the players. And as you will see the great ones are not from a period or an era. They are for all time and transcend the decade or the generation they played in. Yes the great ones would have been great yesterday or today or even tomorrow.

In evaluating the many factors we have tried to remain clinical and objective. We have taken into consideration as many methodological controls as possible. We have always considered first and foremost the total value of the player. The value he presents to his team, his position, his personal playing career. Repeatedly and with much discipline we have asked ourselves many times and in many different subtle ways. Does the player perform the particular skill in a winning capacity? Does he contribute? Does he help? Does he produce?

What can be of greater worth than a guidance of such value?

We kept asking and separating the players by the true indicator that is part of the bone and the marrow of all statistical achievement: *"Does the player provide an advantage to the winning of baseball games?"*

These men therefore are the "winners," both literally and figuratively, of more baseball games than any other players who have ever appeared in a uniform since 1871. We salute them, honor them and praise them. We announce their achievements at this point, following which we will give the charting evaluations of each categorical representation, and the comprehensive rating for them. This will show definitely the integral parts of their great abilities. Those abilities add up to the sum of greatness. The sum that indicates that they are the greatest players and pitchers in the history of the game. It is this ability and the courage that is needed to play this most demanding and challenging of games that is now being recorded.

EDITOR'S NOTE: players have been assigned to the particular teams that they achieved their greatest productivity with. For the current stars teams they currently are with as well as the most productive years they played for are indicated.

**POSITION
PITCHER**

	First Game in Major Leagues (or Years in Major Leagues)	Team	Offensive Total	Defensive Total	Total Rating
All Time Top 27 Starting Pitchers					
Walter Johnson	1907-1927	Wash. Senators			107
Sandy Koufax	1955-1966	L. A. Dodgers			107
Bob "Lefty" Grove	1925-1941	Phila. Athletics			105
Christy Mathewson	1900-1916	N.Y. Giants			103
Grover Cleveland Alexander	1911-1930	Phila. Phils			103
Robert Feller	1936-1956	Cleve. Indians			102
Jay Hanna "Dizzy" Dean	1930-1947	St. L. Cardinals			102
Denton "Cy" Young	1890-1911	Boston Red Sox			100
Warren Spahn	1942-1965	Milwaukee Braves			97
Carl Hubbel	1928-1943	N.Y. Giants			96
Juan Marichal	1960-....	S. F. Giants			95
Charles "Kid" Nichols	1890-1906	Boston Braves			94
Ed "Whitey" Ford	1950-1967	N.Y. Yankees			93
Bob Gibson	1959-....	St. L. Cardinals			93
Clarence "Dazzy" Vance	1915-1935	Brooklyn Dodgers			91
Early Wynn	1939-1962	Cleve. Indians			90
Eddie Plank	1901-1917	Phila. Athletics			89
Charles "Red" Ruffing	1924-1947	N.Y. Yankees			88
Robin Roberts	1948-1966	Phila. Phils			87
Ted Lyons	1923-1946	Chicago White Sox			86
Don Drysdale	1956-....	L. A. Dodgers			86
Herbert Pennock	1912-1934	N.Y. Yankees			83
William "Bucky" Walters	1931-1950	Cin. Reds			82
Bob Lemon	1941-1958	Cleve. Indians			82
Joe "Iron Man" McGinnity	1899-1908	N.Y. Giants			81
Mordecai "Three Fingers" Brown	1903-1913	Chicago Cubs			81
George Edward "Rube" Waddell	1897-1910	Phila. Athletics			81

STARTING PITCHERS
ALL TIME TOP 27

THE SIX PITCHING CATEGORICALS

Rating Scale in points:	1-TEAM VALUE	2-POWER	3-PITCHING ARSENAL VALUE TECHNICAL PROFICIENCY	4-CONTROL	5-EXPERIENCE	6-VERSATILITY AND EXECUTION	TOTAL POINTS
	25	25	20	20	10	10	110 Max (ideal)
WALTER JOHNSON, 1907-1927, Washington Senators	25	25	20	20	10	7	107
SANDY KOUFAX, 1955-1966, L. A. Dodgers	25	25	20	20	10	7	107
BOB "LEFTY" GROVE, 1925-1941, Phila. Athletics	24	24	20	20	10	7	105
CHRISTY MATHEWSON, 1900-1916, N. Y. Giants	24	23	19	20	10	7	103
GROVER CLEVELAND ALEXANDER, 1911-1930, Phila. Phils	24	23	19	20	10	7	103
BOBBY FELLER, 1936-1956, Cleve. Indians	24	24	20	17	10	7	102
JAY HANNA "DIZZY" DEAN, 1930-1947, St. L. Cardinals	24	23	20	19	10	6	102
DENTON "CY" YOUNG, 1890-1911, Boston Red Sox	24	23	18	18	10	7	100
WARREN SPAHN, 1942-1956, Milwaukee Braves	22	18	19	20	10	8	97
CARL "KING" HUBBELL, 1928-1943, N.Y. Giants	22	18	19	20	10	7	96
JUAN MARICHAL, 1960....., S. F. Giants	19	21	18	20	8	9	95
CHARLES 'KID" NICHOLS, 1890-1906, Boston Braves	20	22	17	18	10	7	94
ED "WHITEY" FORD, 1950-1967, N. Y. Yankees	19	18	18	20	10	8	93
BOB "HOOT" GIBSON, 1959....., St. L. Cardinals	19	19	20	17	9	9	93
"DAZZY" VANCE, 1915-1935, Brooklyn Dodgers	19	18	18	18	10	8	91
EARLY WYNN, 1939-1962, Cleve. Indians	18	18	18	18	10	8	90
EDDIE PLANK, 1901-1917, Phila. Athletics	18	18	18	18	10	7	89
CHARLES 'RED" RUFFING, 1924-1947, N. Y. Yankees	18	17	17	17	10	9	88
ROBIN ROBERTS, 1948-1966, Phila. Phils	18	16	16	19	10	8	87

STARTING PITCHERS

ALL TIME TOP 27 (continued)

THE SIX PITCHING CATEGORICALS

Rating Scale in points:	1-TEAM VALUE	2-POWER	3-PITCHING ARSENAL VALUE TECHNICAL PROFICIENCY	4-CONTROL	5-EXPERIENCE	6-VERSATILITY AND EXECUTION	TOTAL POINTS
	25	25	20	20	10	10	110 Max (ideal)
TED LYONS, 1923-1946, Chicago White Sox	17	15	16	18	10	10	86
DON DRYSDALE, 1956-......, L. A. Dodgers	17	15	16	19	10	9	86
HERB PENNOCK, 1912-1934, N.Y. Yankees	16	17	16	17	10	7	83
"BUCKY" WALTERS, 1931-1950, Cin. Reds	15	16	16	17	10	8	82
BOB LEMON, 1941-1958, Cleve. Indians	15	16	16	17	10	8	82
JOE "IRON MAN" MCGINNITY, 1899-1908, N. Y. Giants	15	15	16	17	10	8	81
MORDECAI " THREE FINGER" BROWN, 1903-1916, Chicago Cubs	15	15	16	17	10	8	81
GEORGE "RUBE" WADDELL, 1897-1910, Phila. Athletics	16	16	17	15	10	7	81

POSITION CATCHER

Name	First Game in Major Leagues (or Years in Major Leagues)	Team	Offensive Total	Defensive Total	Total Rating
All Time Top 6 Catchers					
Mickey Cochrane	1925-1937	Phila. Athletics	71	70	141
Bill Dickey	1928-1948	N. Y. Yankees	69	70	139
"Gabby" Hartnett	1922-1941	Chicago Cubs	68	51	119
Larry "Yogi" Berra	1946-1962	N. Y. Yankees	69	50	119
Roy Campanella	1948-1957	Brooklyn Dodgers	61	57	118
Ernie Lombardi	1931-1947	Cin. Reds	67	49	116

POSITION RATED: ALL TIME TOP SIX CATCHERS

	OFFENSIVE CATEGORICALS							DEFENSIVE CATEGORICALS							
	1-TEAM VALUE	2-POWER	3-TECHNICAL PROFICIENCY	4-SPEED	5-EXPERIENCE	6-VERSATILITY AND EXECUTION	THE OFFENSIVE TOTALS	1-TEAM VALUE	2-POWER	3-TECHNICAL PROFICIENCY	4-SPEED	5-EXPERIENCE	6-VERSATILITY AND EXECUTION	THE DEFENSIVE TOTALS	TOTAL POINTS OF PLAYER
Rating Scale in points:	25	25	25	10	10	10	105 Max	20	10	10	10	10	10	70	175 Max (ideal)
Mickey Cochrane, 1925-1937, Phila. Athletics	16	12	16	8	10	9	71	20	10	10	10	10	10	70	141
Bill Dickey, 1928-1946, N. Y. Yankees	15	14	15	8	10	7	69	20	10	10	10	10	10	70	139
Charles "Gabby" Hartnett, 1922-1941, Chicago Cubs	15	16	16	5	10	6	68	15	8	8	5	10	5	51	119
Larry "Yogi" Berra, 1946-1962, N. Y. Yankees	16	17	14	6	10	6	69	15	7	7	6	10	5	50	119
Roy Campanella, 1948-1957, Brooklyn Dodgers	15	17	14	2	10	3	61	16	9	9	5	10	8	57	118
Ernie Lombardi, 1931-1947, Cin. Reds	15	16	20	1	10	5	67	15	7	7	5	10	5	49	116

POSITION
FIRST BASE

	First Game in Major Leagues (or Years in Major Leagues)	Team	Offensive Total	Defensive Total	Total Rating
All Time Top 8					
Lou Gehrig	1923-1939	N. Y. Yankees	96	59	155
George Sisler	1915-1930	St. L. Browns	81	70	151
Bill Terry	1923-1936	N. Y. Giants	82	67	149
Jimmy Foxx	1925-1945	Phila. Athletics	85	49	134
John Mize	1936-1953	St. L. Cardinals and N. Y. Giants	74	50	124
Orlando Cepeda *	1958-....	St. L. Cardinals	71	52	123
Hank Greenberg *	1933-1947	Detroit Tigers	72	51	123
Gill Hodges *	1943-1962	Brooklyn Dodgers	61	62	123

* Cepeda, Greenberg, and Hodges tied for 6th place.

POSITION RATED: ALL TIME TOP EIGHT FIRST BASEMEN

	OFFENSIVE CATEGORICALS							DEFENSIVE CATEGORICALS							
	1-TEAM VALUE	2-POWER	3-TECHNICAL PROFICIENCY	4-SPEED	5-EXPERIENCE	6-VERSATILITY AND EXECUTION	THE OFFENSIVE TOTALS	1-TEAM VALUE	2-POWER	3-TECHNICAL PROFICIENCY	4-SPEED	5-EXPERIENCE	6-VERSATILITY AND EXECUTION	THE DEFENSIVE TOTALS	TOTAL POINTS OF PLAYER
Rating Scale in points:	25	25	25	10	10	10	105 Max	20	10	10	10	10	10	70	175 Max (ideal)
Lou Gehrig, 1923-1939, N. Y. Yankees	23	23	22	8	10	10	96	17	8	8	8	10	8	59	155
George Sisler, 1915-1930, St. L. Browns	17	14	22	8	10	10	81	20	10	10	10	10	10	70	151
Bill Terry, 1923-1936, N. Y. Giants	18	14	23	7	10	10	82	18	10	10	9	10	10	67	149
Jimmy Foxx, 1925-1944, Phila. Athletics	21	22	20	5	10	7	85	13	7	7	5	10	7	49	134
John Mize, 1936-1953, St. L. Cardinals	17	18	19	4	10	6	74	14	7	7	5	10	7	50	124
Orlando Cepeda, 1958-.... St. L. Cardinals	16	16	17	5	10	7	71	14	7	7	7	10	7	52	123
Hank Greenberg, 1933-1947, Detroit Tigers	17	18	17	5	10	5	72	14	7	7	6	10	7	51	123
Gil Hodges, 1943-1962, Brooklyn Dodgers	15	16	11	5	10	4	61	17	9	9	8	10	9	62	123

POSITION
SECOND BASE

	First Game in Major Leagues (or Years in Major Leagues)	Team	Offensive Total	Defensive Total	Total Rating
All Time Top 6					
Rogers Hornsby	1915-1937	St. L. Cardinals	97	52	149
Charles Gehringer	1924-1942	Detroit Tigers	71	70	141
Jackie Robinson	1947-1956	Brooklyn Dodgers	73	62	135
Frank Frisch	1919-1937	St. L. Cardinals	71	61	132
"Napoleon" Larry Lajoie	1896-1916	Cleve. Indians	74	54	128
Eddie Collins	1906-1930	Phila. Athletics and Chicago White Sox	73	54	127

POSITION RATED: ALL TIME TOP SIX SECOND BASEMEN

	OFFENSIVE CATEGORICALS							DEFENSIVE CATEGORICALS							
	1-TEAM VALUE	2-POWER	3-TECHNICAL PROFICIENCY	4-SPEED	5-EXPERIENCE	6-VERSATILITY AND EXECUTION	THE OFFENSIVE TOTALS	1-TEAM VALUE	2-POWER	3-TECHNICAL PROFICIENCY	4-SPEED	5-EXPERIENCE	6-VERSATILITY AND EXECUTION	THE DEFENSIVE TOTALS	TOTAL POINTS OF PLAYER
Rating Scale in points:	25	25	25	10	10	10	105 Max	20	10	10	10	10	10	70	175 Max (ideal)
Rogers Hornsby, 1915-1937, St. L. Cardinals	22	20	25	10	10	10	97	13	7	7	8	10	7	52	149
Charles Gehringer, 1924-1942, Detroit Tigers	14	13	16	9	10	9	71	20	10	10	10	10	10	70	141
Jackie Robinson, 1947-1956, Brooklyn Dodgers	15	14	15	10	10	9	73	17	8	8	9	10	10	62	135
Frank Frisch, 1919-1937, N.Y. Giants & St. L. Cardinals	14	12	15	10	10	10	71	16	8	8	9	10	10	61	132
Larry "Napoleon" Lajoie, 1896-1916, Cleve. Indians	15	12	17	10	10	10	74	13	7	7	9	10	8	54	128
Eddie Collins, 1909-1930, Phila. Athletics & Chi. White Sox	14	12	17	10	10	10	73	13	7	7	9	10	8	54	127

POSITION SHORTSTOP

	First Game in Major Leagues (or Years in Major Leagues)	Team	Offensive Total	Defensive Total	Total Rating
All Time Top 7					
Honus Wagner	1897-1917	Pit. Pirates	86	70	156
Ernie Banks	1953-....	Chicago Cubs	74	45	119
Luke Appling	1936-1950	Chicago White Sox	62	54	116
Joe Cronin	1926-1950	Boston Red Sox	56	56	112
Phil "Scooter" Rizzuto	1941-1956	N.Y. Yankees	49	63	112
Walter "Rabbit" Maranville *	1912-1935	Boston Braves	48	63	111
Maury Wills *	1959-....	L. A. Dodgers and Montreal Expos and Pit. Pirates	64	47	111

* Maranville and Wills tied for 6th place in all time shortstop position.

POSITION RATED: ALL TIME TOP SEVEN SHORTSTOPS

	OFFENSIVE CATEGORICALS							DEFENSIVE CATEGORICALS							
	1-TEAM VALUE	2-POWER	3-TECHNICAL PROFICIENCY	4-SPEED	5-EXPERIENCE	6-VERSATILITY AND EXECUTION	THE OFFENSIVE TOTALS	1-TEAM VALUE	2-POWER	3-TECHNICAL PROFICIENCY	4-SPEED	5-EXPERIENCE	6-VERSATILITY AND EXECUTION	THE DEFENSIVE TOTALS	TOTAL POINTS OF PLAYER
Rating Scale in points:	25	25	25	10	10	10	105 Max	20	10	10	10	10	10	70	175 Max (ideal)
Honus Wagner, 1897-1917, Pit. Pirates	19	17	20	10	10	10	86	20	10	10	10	10	10	70	156
Ernie Banks, 1953-...., Chicago Cubs	18	19	15	6	10	6	74	12	6	6	5	10	6	45	119
Luke Appling, 1936-1950, Chicago White Sox	13	10	13	6	10	10	62	15	8	7	7	10	7	54	116
Joe Cronin, 1926-1945, Boston Red Sox	12	10	12	5	10	7	56	14	8	8	8	10	8	56	112
Phil 'Scooter" Rizzuto, 1941-1956, N.Y. Yankees	9	5	10	8	10	7	49	17	8	8	10	10	10	63	112
Walter "Rabbit" Maranville, 1912-1935, Boston Braves	8	5	10	8	10	7	48	17	8	8	10	10	10	63	111
Maurey Wills, 1959-...., Montreal Expos	16	8	10	10	10	10	64	10	6	6	8	10	7	47	111

POSITION
THIRD BASE

	First Game in Major Leagues (or Years in Major Leagues)	Team	Offensive Total	Defensive Total	Total Rating
All Time Top 7					
Harold "Pie" Traynor	1920-1937	Pit. Pirates	67	70	137
Brooks Robinson	1957-....	Balt. Orioles	58	70	128
Ed Mathews	1952-1968	Milw. Braves	73	46	119
Ron Santo	1960-....	Chicago Cubs	61	57	118
Ken Boyer	1955-....	St. L. Cardinals and L. A. Dodgers	60	58	118
George Kell *	1943-1957	Detroit Tigers	57	56	113
John J. McGraw *	1891-1906	Balt. Orioles and N. Y. Giants	61	52	113

* Kell and McGraw tied for 6th place in all time third base ratings.

POSITION RATED: ALL TIME TOP SEVEN THIRD BASEMEN

	OFFENSIVE CATEGORICALS							DEFENSIVE CATEGORICALS							
	1-TEAM VALUE	2-POWER	3-TECHNICAL PROFICIENCY	4-SPEED	5-EXPERIENCE	6-VERSATILITY AND EXECUTION	THE OFFENSIVE TOTALS	1-TEAM VALUE	2-POWER	3-TECHNICAL PROFICIENCY	4-SPEED	5-EXPERIENCE	6-VERSATILITY AND EXECUTION	THE DEFENSIVE TOTALS	TOTAL POINTS OF PLAYER
Rating Scale in points:	25	25	25	10	10	10	105 Max	20	10	10	10	10	10	70	175 Max (ideal)
Harold "Pie" Traynor, 1920-1937, Pit. Pirates	15	12	16	6	10	8	67	20	10	10	10	10	10	70	137
Brooks Robinson, 1957-...., Baltimore Orioles	13	12	13	5	10	5	58	20	10	10	10	10	10	70	128
Ed Mathews, 1952-1968, Milw. & Atlanta Braves	17	19	14	7	10	6	73	10	7	7	7	9	6	46	119
Ron Santo, 1960-...., Chicago Cubs	16	15	14	5	7	5	62	16	8	8	8	8	8	56	118
Ken Boyer, 1955-...., St. L. Cardinals & L.A. Dodgers	13	14	13	5	10	5	60	16	8	8	8	10	8	58	118
George Kell, 1943-1957, Detroit Tigers	13	10	13	5	10	6	57	15	8	8	7	10	8	56	113
John J. McGraw, 1891-1906, Balt. Orioles & N.Y. Giants	15	7	16	6	10	7	61	14	7	7	7	10	7	52	113

POSITION: LEFT FIELD

	First Game in Major Leagues (or Years in Major Leagues)	Team	Offensive Total	Defensive Total	Total Rating
All Time Top 6					
Tyrus "Ty" Cobb	1905-1928	Detroit Tigers	98	62	160
Ted "The Thumper" Williams	1939-1960	Boston Red Sox	101	52	153
Stan "The Man" Musial	1941-1962	St. L. Cardinals	94	51	145
Al "Bucket Foot" Simmons	1924-1940	Phila. Athletics	81	48	129
"Shoeless" Joe Jackson	1908-1920	Cleve. Indians and Chicago White Sox	89	40	129
William "Wee Willie" Keeler	1892-1910	Brooklyn Dodgers	82	47	129

POSITION RATED: ALL TIME TOP SIX LEFT FIELDERS

	OFFENSIVE CATEGORICALS							DEFENSIVE CATEGORICALS							
	1-TEAM VALUE	2-POWER	3-TECHNICAL PROFICIENCY	4-SPEED	5-EXPERIENCE	6-VERSATILITY AND EXECUTION	THE OFFENSIVE TOTALS	1-TEAM VALUE	2-POWER	3-TECHNICAL PROFICIENCY	4-SPEED	5-EXPERIENCE	6-VERSATILITY AND EXECUTION	THE DEFENSIVE TOTALS	TOTAL POINTS OF PLAYER
Rating Scale in points:	25	25	25	10	10	10	105 Max	20	10	10	10	10	10	70	175 Max (ideal)
Tyrus "Ty" Raymond Cobb, 1905-1928, Detroit Tigers	23	20	25	10	10	10	98	18	7	7	10	10	10	62	160
Ted "Thumper" Williams, 1939-1960, Boston Red Sox	25	25	25	6	10	10	101	15	7	7	5	10	8	52	153
Stan "The Man" Musial, 1941-1962, St. L. Cardinals	22	23	22	7	10	10	94	14	7	7	6	10	7	51	145
Al "Bucketfoot" Simmons, 1924-1940, Phila. Athletics	18	18	20	7	10	8	81	13	7	7	5	10	6	48	129
"Shoeless" Joe Jackson 1908-1920, Cleve. & Chi. White Sox	18	16	25	10	10	10	89	10	5	5	5	10	5	40	129
William "Wee Willie" Keeler 1892-1910, Brooklyn Dodgers	18	11	23	10	10	10	82	10	6	5	8	10	8	47	129

POSITION CENTERFIELD

	First Game in Major Leagues (or Years in Major Leagues)	Team	Offensive Total	Defensive Total	Total Rating
All Time Top 6					
Joe DiMaggio "The Yankee Clipper"	1936-1951	N.Y. Yankees	92	70	162
Willie Mays	1951-....	S. F. Giants	91	70	161
Tris Speaker "The Grey Eagle"	1907-1928	Cleve. Indians	85	70	155
Mickey Mantle	1951-....	N.Y. Yankees	92	56	148
Edd J. Roush	1913-1931	Cin. Reds	81	59	140
Edwin "Duke" Snider	1947-1962	Brooklyn Dodgers	71	59	130

POSITION RATED: ALL TIME TOP SIX CENTER FIELDERS

	OFFENSIVE CATEGORICALS							DEFENSIVE CATEGORICALS							
	1-TEAM VALUE	2-POWER	3-TECHNICAL PROFICIENCY	4-SPEED	5-EXPERIENCE	6-VERSATILITY AND EXECUTION	THE OFFENSIVE TOTALS	1-TEAM VALUE	2-POWER	3-TECHNICAL PROFICIENCY	4-SPEED	5-EXPERIENCE	6-VERSATILITY AND EXECUTION	THE DEFENSIVE TOTALS	TOTAL POINTS OF PLAYER
Rating Scale in points:	25	25	25	10	10	10	105 Max	20	10	10	10	10	10	70	175 Max (ideal)
Joe DiMaggio, 1936-1951, N.Y. Yankees	25	20	22	7	10	8	92	20	10	10	10	10	10	70	162
Willie Mays, 1951-...., S. F. Giants	23	23	19	8	10	8	91	20	10	10	10	10	10	70	161
Tris Speaker, 1907-1928, Cleveland Indians	19	15	22	9	10	10	85	20	10	10	10	10	10	70	155
Mickey Mantle, 1951-...., N.Y. Yankees	23	23	19	10	10	7	92	15	7	7	10	10	7	56	148
Edd J. Roush, 1913-1931 Cin. Reds	18	18	19	8	10	8	81	17	8	8	8	10	8	59	140
Edwin "Duke" Snider, 1947-1962, Brooklyn Dodgers	18	18	14	6	10	5	71	17	8	8	8	10	8	59	130

POSITION
RIGHT FIELD

All Time Top 6

	First Game in Major Leagues (or Years in Major Leagues)	Team	Offensive Total	Defensive Total	Total Rating
George Herman "Babe" Ruth	1914-1935	N.Y. Yankees	101	62	163 *
Hank "Bad Henry" Aaron	1954-....	Atlanta Braves	88	62	150
Harry Heilmann	1914-1932	Detroit Tigers	87	56	143
Mel Ott	1926-1947	N.Y. Giants	83	59	142
Roberto Clemente	1955-....	Pit. Pirates	71	64	135
Paul "Big Poison" Waner	1926-1945	Pit. Pirates	76	57	133

* Ruth's total of 163 points is the highest player score of the rating system's analysis.

POSITION RATED: ALL TIME TOP SIX RIGHT FIELDERS

	OFFENSIVE CATEGORICALS							DEFENSIVE CATEGORICALS							
	1-TEAM VALUE	2-POWER	3-TECHNICAL PROFICIENCY	4-SPEED	5-EXPERIENCE	6-VERSATILITY AND EXECUTION	THE OFFENSIVE TOTALS	1-TEAM VALUE	2-POWER	3-TECHNICAL PROFICIENCY	4-SPEED	5-EXPERIENCE	6-VERSATILITY AND EXECUTION	THE DEFENSIVE TOTALS	TOTAL POINTS OF PLAYER
Rating Scale in points:	25	25	25	10	10	10	105 Max	20	10	10	10	10	10	70	175 Max (ideal)
George Herman "Babe" Ruth, 1914-1935, N.Y. Yankees	25	25	25	6	10	10	101	17	9	9	8	10	9	62	163
Hank Aaron, 1954-...., Atlanta Braves	21	20	21	8	10	8	88	17	9	8	9	10	9	62	150
Harry Heilmann, 1914-1932, Detroit Tigers	18	17	22	10	10	10	87	17	7	8	7	10	7	56	143
Mel Ott, 1926-1947, N.Y. Giants	20	21	18	8	10	6	83	17	8	8	8	10	8	59	142
Roberto Clemente, 1955-...., Pit. Pirates	16	15	15	7	10	8	71	18	9	9	9	10	9	64	135
Paul Waner, 1926-1945, Pit. Pirates	14	13	20	9	10	10	76	15	8	8	8	10	8	57	133

2

Profiles on the All Time Greats

Below is a short (sometimes very short) profile of some of the achievements of the all time greats.

PITCHERS. (27)

Christy Mathewson ("Matty," "Big Six") (1900–1916): N.Y. Giants

From 1903 through 1914 he won 20 or more games in each season. That comes to 12 consecutive 20 game seasons, and no one has ever done better. "Matty" was a great performer, winning 373 games in all and invariably all the big ones, including the precious World Series games he was asked to pitch in.

Grover Cleveland ("Pete") Alexander (1907-1922): Philadelphia Phils

Won, as "Matty" did 373 games including a 28 and 11 rookie season in 1911. That was his rookie year, Mel, how about that! In 1915 he led the league in strikeouts with 241 and also won 31 games and compiled an earned run average of 1.22. The wins and the E.R.A. had not been surpassed until McLain and Gibson tried. Did they succeed, folks?

True Denton ("Cy") Young (1890-1911):

In the early years for Cleveland and later on for St. Louis (National) and Boston (American), he won more games than any pitcher in the game's history—507 to be exact. He lost 200 less games, and in all appeared in close to 1000 major league games.

George Edward ("Rube") Waddell (1897-1910): Philadelphia Athletics:

Rube had one of the greatest arms of any left hander in the history of baseball. He led the American League in strikeouts in seven different seasons—still a major league record. In 1903 he struck out 301 men and in 1904 343. Until Koufax came around these were standout records for every left hander. Mr. Mack was his manager and he always referred to the lefthander with affection. Even 50 years after Rube left the scene Connie was still singing his praise. Twice Rube won 26 games in a season, in 1904 and 1905. In all, this great won 197 major league games. He had the fast ball.

Walter Johnson ("The Big Train") (1907–1927):
Washington Senators

Performed his entire career for the humble Washington club. With this chronic second division team he was still the winner of 414 games while losing only 281. He is still the holder of many of the all-time strikeout records. "Barney" had the one pitch—the fast ball. And it was fast, probably the fastest in history.

Bob ("Lefty") Grove (1925–1941): Philadelphia Athletics

For beginners won 28 games while losing only five in 1930. The following year he won 31 and lost 4. For his career he won 300 while losing the amazingly low total of 141. Has the unbelievable record of leading the league in E.R.A. 9 different years—a major league record.

Carl ("King") Hubbell (1928–1943): N.Y. Giants:

Pitched for the Giants during his entire career. With that screwball he won 253 games and once struck out some players in an all star game. They included Ruth and Gehrig and Foxx and etc., etc. I think the point is made.

Eddie Plank (1901–1917): Philadelphia Athletics

Winner of 326 games, mainly for the Athletics. Connie Mack thought of him when he said "pitching is 90 per cent of the game."

Bobby ("Rapid Robert") Feller (1936–1956: Cleveland Indians

Winner of 266 games. Holder of strikeout records,

three no hitters, and nine one hitters. If you missed his fast ball, you missed only a blur.

Jay Hanna ("Dizzy") Dean (1930–1947): St. Louis Cardinals

Because of injury his career was cut short at its height. But he was one of the greats, the winner of 30 games in 1934. He was probably the most "colorful" pitcher in major league history.

Clarence Arthur ("Dazzy") Vance (1915–1935): Brooklyn Dodgers

Winner of 197 games for the chronic 2nd division Dodgers. One of the best fast balls in major league history.

Herb Pennock (1912–1934): N.Y. Yankees

Winner of 243 games, and many of them big ones. Crafty and classy.

Warren Spahn (1942–1965): Boston-Milwaukee Braves

Winner of 363 games in his career. Some thought this great left hander would be winning 20 at 50. He came close.

Early ("Gus") Wynn (1939–1962): Cleveland Indians

Winner of 301 games and always known as the "fiercest" competitor in the game. They say he would have knocked down his mother to win a game, and he would have.

Sanford ("Sandy") Koufax (1955–1965): L.A. Dodgers

Always can be considered the best example of what hard work and discipline can do for a pitcher. He possessed a great fast ball and curve, but only after many years did he perfect the control necessary to win with these bullets. During his great career for the "no hitting" Dodgers, he won every big game, had the greatest E.R.A., each season, pitched three no hitters, and broke every season strikeout mark. Truly the greatest of modern pitchers. Who can ever forget him?

Mordecai ("Three Fingers") Brown (1903–1916): Chicago Cubs

Winner of 238 games. A great competitor.

Edward ("Whitey") Ford (1950–1967): N.Y. Yankees

The winner of 236 games and the loser only 106. A great gutsy little guy, and possessor of many World Series records; and when the pennant was on the line the word always was, "give the ball to Whitey."

Joe ("Iron Man") McGinnity (1899–1908): N.Y. Giants

In 1904 he compiled a record of 35–8. In all he won 247 games and was one of the strong men of the game. A great and determined athlete.

William ("Bucky") Walters (1931–1950): Cincinnatti Reds

Winner of 198 games, a great competitor who pitched mainly with a second division team. Also played some infield before going to the mound.

Bob Lemon (1941–1958): Cleveland Indians

This winner of 207 games, like Walters made the switch to the mound after coming to the big leagues as an infielder. His pitches "moved" even in warm ups before the game.

Ted Lyons (1923–1946): Chicago White Sox

Winner of 260 games for the Chicago club. One of the most knowledgeable men of the art of pitching in the game's history.

Robin Roberts (1948–1966): Philadelphia Phils

The winner of 28 games in one season, and the winner of 20 games for six straight years. One of the great control pitchers in modern era.

Charles Augustus ("Kid") Nichols (1890–1906): Boston, St. Louis, and Philadelphia (N)

Many years ago when pitchers were made of iron and could pitch and pitch and pitch, Nichols was one of them. He had seven seasons in which he won 30 or more games. In all he won 361 games in his career and appeared in over 700 professional ball games. The "Kid" was one of the first of the great pitchers.

Charles ("Red") Ruffing (1924–1947): N.Y. Yankees

"Red" won 273 games in his career. He was also one of the best hitting pitchers in the game's history. During his great years with the Yankees he had four consecutive 20 game win seasons. They were in '36, '37, '38, and '39. He pitched for almost a quarter of a century, and he pitched to win.

Juan Marichal (1960): San Francisco Giants
Bob Gibson (1959): St. Louis Cardinals
Don Drysdale (1956): Los Angeles Dodgers

These great stars are still going every four days. They are also still winning, and represent the greatest in the game today as well as rating formidably with the greatest in the game's history. Marichal completes almost every game he's in, and his overall record will be truly unbelievable.

Gibson wins the big ones, and in '68 he was on the same level with Koufax and Johnson.

Drysdale pitches in rotation, and he wins and wins and wins. Over a career he did more for the Dodgers than Koufax. Look it up.

PROFILES ON THE ALL TIME GREAT CATCHERS

Gordon ("Mickey") Cochrane (1925-1937): Philadelphia Athletics

Lifetime batting average of .320. Great defensive catcher and what a competitor!

William ("Bill") Dickey (1928-1946): N.Y. Yankees

Lifetime batting average of .313. He hit 202 home runs and was a classy defensive player.

Charles ("Gabby") Hartnett (1922-1941): Chicago Cubs

He hit 236 home runs, and had a solid .298 lifetime B.A. He also could direct the pitcher, and hit in the clutch.

Larry ("Yogi") Berra (1946–1962): N.Y. Yankees

Hit 358 lifetime home runs, most in the position's history. In the clutch there was none better. Even Early Wynn was careful, maybe afraid of him.

Roy Campanella (1948–1957): Brooklyn Dodgers

He belted 242 home runs, winner of the most valuable player award, in his prime. Great knowledge of the game, and exceptional with young pitchers.

Ernie ("Schnozz") Lombardi (1931–1947): Cincinnati Reds

Lifetime batting average of .306. If it wasn't for his lack of speed, he would have hit .350—ask Ted Williams.

PROFILES ON THE ALL TIME GREAT FIRST BASEMEN

Lou Gehrig ("The Iron Horse") (1923–1939): N.Y. Yankees

Lifetime batting average of .340, with 493 home runs. But his value was more. He played every day, with hurts, pains and fevers. He had the demeanor that was wanted in a ball player. He was a gentleman and personified the winning ball player.

Jimmy ("Double X") Foxx (1925–1945): Philadelphia Athletics

534 lifetime home runs, and batting average for career of .325. The power of a Mantle.

William (Bill) Terry (1923–1936): N.Y. Giants

Lifetime batting average of .341. Great defense, and could hit with anyone.

George Sisler (1915–1930): St. Louis Browns

Lifetime of .341 and best defense at position in game's history.

John Mize ("Big Jawn," "Big Cat") (1936–1953): St. Louis Cardinals, N.Y. Giants

Mize had a .313 lifetime batting average, with 359 home runs. Could hit a baseball with artistry. Another of the all too rare "perfect hitters."

Hank ("Hammerin Henry") Greenberg (1933–1947): Detroit Tigers

Greenberg swatted 331 lifetime home runs. He hit 58 in one year; and then they walked him. . .

Gil Hodges (1943–1962): Brooklyn Dodgers

He hit 355 home runs and don't forget those Runs Batted In, and that defense too.

Orlando Cepeda ("The Baby Bull") (1958–) St. Louis Cardinals:

One of the great sluggers in the game today, still producing "par excellence" and with a lifetime batting average of .302. He's already going for his 300th homerun. The Most Valuable Player in National League in 1967.

PROFILES ON THE ALL TIME GREAT SECOND BASEMEN

Rogers ("The Rajah") Hornsby (1915–1937): **St. Louis Cardinals**

Greatest right hand hitter in game's history. Why? . . . a .358 lifetime average, and with power also—300 home runs. A perfect swing, he hit line drives almost every time.

Eddie Collins (1906–1930): Chicago White Sox and Philadelphia Athletics

He played for 25 years. He was a lifetime batter of .333. And he also was able to get 3313 hits, and remain in 2826 major league games. 744 lifetime stolen bases. Great speed for Mr. Collins.

Jackie Robinson (1947–1956): Brooklyn Dodgers

Lifetime batting average of .311. A great competitor, and he had the courage, intelligence and class that should connote major leaguer. His base running was as good as a no hitter.

Larry ("Napoleon") Lajoie (1896–1916): Cleveland Indians

Lifetime batting average of .339. He hit .422 in 1901. Played in 2475 major league games.

Frankie Frisch ("Fordham flash") (1919–1937): **St. Louis Cardinals and N.Y. Giants**

Heart, hustle and guts. Besides, he hit .316 for a lifetime and could field and run and manage—and give advice too.

Charles Gehringer (1924–1942): Detroit Tigers

In Detroit they won't even talk about his bat, and it was good, (.321 lifetime). They speak reverently about his glove, which was the best in the position's history.

PROFILES ON THE ALL TIME GREAT SHORTSTOPS

John ("Honus") Wagner (1897–1917): Pittsburgh Pirates

Lifetime of .329, could run and hit with power. His glove was what made him a genius. The complete ball player. Over 500 steals.

Ernie Banks (1953–) Chicago Cubs

Going for 500 home runs, and those R.B.I.'s also. Greatest power hitter in position's history. Most Valuable Player awards in '58 and '59.

Joe Cronin (1926–1945): Boston Red Sox

Lifetime of .302. Played defense, and was a great competitor.

Luke Appling ("Old Aches and Pains") (1930–1950): Chicago White Sox

Lifetime batting average of .310. Defense and bat control and a winner.

Phil ("Scooter") Rizzuto (1941–1956): N.Y. Yankees

His glove was as pretty as any in the game's history. No arm, but he made all the plays, and some that you shouldn't make. A great competitor. And what a bunter. His enthusiasm was "beautiful."

Walter ("Rabbit") Maranville (1912–1935): Boston Braves

Played in 2670 major league games. He was known for his glove and speed. He will remain known for his glove and speed.

Maury (Mouse) Wills (1959–): L.A. Dodgers, Pittsburgh Pirates, Montreal Expos

Maury has a lifetime batting average of .288. He is the greatest base stealer in the game since Ty Cobb. He broke Cobb's record of 96 with a fantastic 104 in 1962. At this time he has reached his 500th stolen base. He would beat you with his speed, and his guts and his intelligence. Getting back to those "500" steals only Hall of Famers Cobb, Wagner, Eddie Collins and Max Carey have more. Only Carey did it with the catcher directly in back of the plate, the others, including Cobb, did it when the catcher caught the ball on a bounce from eight feet back of the batter. Yes Maury could run and steal with anyone.

PROFILES ON THE ALL TIME GREAT THIRD BASEMEN

John J. McGraw ("little Napoleon") 1891–1906): Baltimore Orioles and N.Y. Giants

Guts, courage and that "Old Oriole" spirit made him what he was. Before he managed he could play with the best of them. And even in those days a .334 lifetime batting average meant you knew how to use the wood.

George Kell (1943–1957): Detroit Tigers

Classy third baseman who could hit and field. He battled "The Thumper" for a few batting crowns and he once had his jaw broken on a DiMaggio smash. His lifetime average was .306, and his hits and glove won ball games.

Ron Santo (1960–): Chicago Cubs

This youngster can do everything wanted of a ball player. He captains the Cubbies now, and hits like a general. Will be adding impressive statistics to the home run score and R.B.I. lists before he hangs up the glove. Has all of the ability and all of the quiet of a winner.

Ken Boyer (1955–): St. Louis Cardinals, N.Y. Mets, L.A. Dodgers

Now at the twilight of a great career, Ken was a Cardinal for years. A great glove and solid clutch hitter who could beat you both ways. Had a .290 lifetime batting average, and over 300 home runs.

Ed Mathews (1952–1968): Milwaukee–Atlanta Braves

The greatest home run hitter in the position's history, with over 500 to date. For the "long ball" he could hit with anyone and did his job with the glove also. When he played with Aaron in Milwaukee they formed the most powerful one-two punch since Gehrig and Ruth. Over 1000 home runs for A. & M.—and most of them were hit for the same team.

Brooks Robinson (1957–): Baltimore Orioles

Came to play with the Orioles in '57. He has been considered the greatest defender of the "hot corner" in the game's history. If you have seen him do his magic you know why. His reputation as a solid hitter is for real also. He's a clutch hitter and can go for the home run also.

Harold ("Pie") Traynor (1920–1937): Pittsburgh Pirates

A lifetime hitter of .320. Defensively maybe the best in the game's history. They compare Brooks to him and that says everything.

PROFILES ON THE ALL TIME GREAT LEFT FIELDERS

Tyrus Raymond ("Ty") Cobb (1905–1928): Detroit Tigers

The Georgia Peach had a lifetime batting average of .367. No one ever did better. He was the "most" competitor in the game's history, its greatest base runner, and its greatest. . . . The system says Ruth. His 892 lifetime stolen bases is a major league record.

Ted Williams ("The Thumper") (1939–1960): Boston Red Sox

It was a privilege to see him hit. He had a lifetime average of .344 and he parked 521 home runs. He left the game after his last. Always a perfectionist, he was the most perfect hitter you could ever witness. Better than a blueprint. "I would want him at the plate all the time. . . ."

Al ("Bucketfoot") Simmons (1924–1940): Philadelphia Athletics

Played in 2215 games with a lifetime batting average of .334. He also could hit the long one—330 home runs.

"Shoeless" Joe Jackson (1908–1920): Cleveland Indians and Chicago White Sox

Ruth said Joe was the best hitter he ever saw. He was almost perfect with a career batting average of .356.

William ("Wee Willie") Keeler (1892–1910): Brooklyn Dodgers

Performed way back when. He could "hit them where they ain't" as good as anybody, as his .345 lifetime mark will attest to. Way back, say 1897, he hit them where they weren't at a .432 clip. Played in 2119 games.

Stan ("The Man") Musial (1941–1962): St. Louis Cardinals

Lifetime batting average of .331. His 475 home runs. His records for hitting could fill the pages of this book. He had more than most, he had real class. A gentleman.

PROFILES ON THE ALL TIME GREAT CENTER FIELDERS

"Joltin' Joe DiMaggio (1936–1951): N.Y. Yankees

The Yankee Clipper left when Mantle came up. The possessor of the great consecutive game hitting streak of 56 straight games. A .325 lifetime batting average and perfect on defense, and a great home run hitter. Joe D. was the complete ball player and has the second highest rating total of any player by the six categoricals. "The Yankee Clipper" had everything. He wore "Number five."

Willie Mays (1951–): S.F. Giants

"Say hey" what can't he do? Still hitting home runs, making the plays, and exciting fans. He received the third highest rating with 161 points. He's going for 600 home runs and his overall play can be spelled G.E.N.I.U.S.

Edd J. Roush (1913–1931): Cincinnati Reds

Played in 1967 games and maintained a lifetime batting average of .323. His glove and speed were exceptional.

Edwin ("Duke") Snider (1947–1962): Brooklyn Dodgers

Was a real Brooklyn "bum" as he was "The Duke" to all of Flatbush. His lifetime batting average was .300. His 389 home runs were hit all over, and many times into Bedford Avenue. He also played defense and many said "Mantle, Mays, and Snider, and they then asked, "Who's the best?"

Mickey Charles Mantle (1951–): N.Y. Yankees

One of the great competitors in the game's history. Still a great long ball threat, and in his youth he could run with anyone. Going for 600 home runs and has already achieved 1500 R.B.I.'s And only The Babe and Ted Williams had more bases on balls.

Tris Speaker ("The Grey Eagle") (1907–1928): Cleveland Indians

He could do it all. Lifetime of .344. On defense he covered as much ground as anyone. Played a very short center, but went back on a ball like DiMag.

PROFILES ON THE ALL TIME GREAT RIGHT-FIELDERS

George Herman ("Babe") Ruth (1914–1935): N.Y. Yankees

Lifetime batting average of .342. Hit 714 career home runs. And he was the most ball player who ever lived. The rating system gives him 163 points out of 175—the most of anyone. Very likely it's the most of all time. The Bambino was the Yankees, and all of baseball loved him. By the way he came close to making the top 25 pitcher list also.

Mel Ott (1926–1947): N.Y. Giants

He came to the Giants at the age of 17. He played for a generation and his accomplishments included 511 home runs and 1708 bases on balls; three had more— Ruth, Williams and Mantle. His lifetime batting average was solid .304. He belongs.

Harry Heilmann (1914–1932): Detroit Tigers

Came up to the Tigers the same year that the Boston Red Sox called up a young pitcher named Ruth. He also stayed for awhile. His batting average for a career was .342. What else do you have to know?

Henry ("Bad Henry") Aaron (1954–): Atlanta Braves

"Bad Henry" has the "sweetest wrists" in the game. He's only 175 lbs. but like "the sugar man" of boxing he might be pound for pound the greatest of them all. Lifetime batting average of .316, and also going for 600 career home runs.

Roberto Clemente (1955–): Pittsburgh Pirates

Lifetime he has won more batting crowns than such contemporaries as Mays, Mantle, and Aaron. His lifetime mark is .316. He is the kind of right fielder you would pay to see play defense.

Paul ("Big Poison") Waner (1926–1945): Pittsburgh Pirates

Played in 2549 major league games, and had 3152 hits. Eighth best of all time. His career batting average was .333. He could run and he could field and he could also win. His brother Lloyd "Little Poison" Waner came close in the ratings.

3

The Six Categorical Rating System's Selection of the All Time All Star Teams

The teams of the players selected are based on the factor of productivity. The team player had best years with is the team identified with player.

THE RATING SYSTEMS ALL TIME
MAJOR LEAGUE FIRST TEAM:

Position	Player	Team	Total Points
Pitcher			
Right Hander	Walter Johnson	Wash. Senators	107
Left Hander	Sandy Koufax	L.A. Dodgers	107

Position	Player	Team	Total Points
Catcher	Mickey Cochrane	Phila. Athletics	141
First Base	Lou Gehrig	N.Y. Yankees	155
Second Base	Rogers Hornsby	St.L. Cardinals	149
Third Base	"Pie" Traynor	Pit. Pirates	137
Short Stop	Honus Wagner	Pit. Pirates	156
Left Field	Ty Cobb	Det. Tigers	160
Center Field	Joe DiMaggio	N.Y. Yankees	162
Right Field	George Herman Ruth	N.Y. Yankees	163

SECOND TEAM:

Position	Player	Team	Total Points
Pitcher			
Right Hander	Christy Mathewson	N.Y. Giants	103
Left Hander	Bob "Lefty" Grove	Phila. Athletics	105
Catcher	Bill Dickey	N.Y. Yankees	139
First Base	George Sisler	St.L. Browns	151
Second Base	Charlie Gehringer	Det. Tigers	149
Third Base	Brooks Robinson	Balt. Orioles	128
Short Stop	Ernie Banks	Chicago Cubs	119
Left Field	Ted Williams	Boston Red Sox	153
Center Field	Willie Mays	S.F. Giants	161
Right Field	Hank Aaron	Atlanta Braves	150

THIRD TEAM:

Position	Player	Team	Total Points
Pitcher			
Right Hander	Grover Cleveland Alexander	Phila. Athletics	103
Left Hander	Warren Spahn	Milw. Braves	97
Catcher	* Larry "Yogi" Berra	N.Y. Yankees	119
First Base	Bill Terry	N.Y. Giants	149
Second Base	Jackie Robinson	Brooklyn Dodgers	135
Third Base	Ed Mathews	Milw. Braves	119

Short Stop	Luke Appling	Chicago White Sox	116
Left Field	Stan "The Man" Musial	St.L. Cardinals	145
Center Field	Tris "The Grey Eagle" Speaker	Cleve. Indians	155
Right Field	Harry Heilmann	Det. Tigers	143

FOURTH TEAM:

Position	Player	Team	Total Points
Pitcher			
Right Hander	Bobby Feller	Cleve. Indians	102
Left Hander	Carl Hubbell	N.Y. Giants	96
Catcher	* "Gabby" Harnett	Chi. Cubs	119
First Base	Jimmy Foxx	Phila. Athletics	134
Second Base	Frank Frisch	St.L. Cardinals	132
Third Base	** Ron Santo	Chicago Cubs	118
Short Stop	Joe Cronin	Boston Red Sox	112
Left Field	Al Simmons	Phila. Athletics	129
Center Field	Mickey Mantle	N.Y. Yankees	148
Right Field	Mel Ott	N.Y. Giants	142

FIFTH TEAM:

Position	Player	Team	Total Points
Pitcher			
Right Hander	Jay Hanna "Dizzy" Dean	St.L. Cardinals	102
Left Hander	Edward "Whitey" Ford	N.Y. Yankees	93
Catcher	Roy Campanella	Brooklyn Dodgers	118
First Base	John Mize	St.L. Cardinals	124
Second Base	Larry "Napoleon" Lajoie	Cleve. Indians	128
Third Base	** Ken Boyer	St.L. Cardinals	118

* Berra and Hartnett had 119 each in rating. But Berra had more Offensive points.
** Santo and Boyer each had 118 points in ratings, but Santo with additional experience will increase his totals.

Short Stop	Phil "Scooter" Rizzuto	N.Y. Yankees	112
Left Field	"Shoeless" Joe Jackson	Chi. White Sox	129
Center Field	Edd J. Roush	Cin. Reds	140
Right Field	Roberto Clemente	Pit. Pirates	135

4

The Legend Makers: The Greatest of the Long Ball Hitters

Who are the men who hit the longest home runs? And who hit them with the most consistency? These questions have been asked and debated by fans for many years. The long ball hitters have fascinated the fan and given more glamor to the game than any other ingredient. Probably the real debates started soon after 1919. That was the year The "Bambino" played regularly and broke all records with an amazing 29 home runs. The following year "The Babe" and the long ball became even more famous as he hit an impossible 54 out of the park.

Since that time many players have hit long home runs, and many have hit them with consistency. The legends of the prowess of these players will last and grow with the passing of time. Many fans will be saying, "I saw the one hit over 500 feet by . . . " The legends and stories will grow, of that I am sure.

Well the long ball hitters are not only stories they are real flesh and blood men of the game and here I will list those I think deserve the highest ranking for this particular achievement in the entire history of the game.

1: MICKEY CHARLES MANTLE: N.Y. YANKEES 1951–

As of now Mick has hit over 500 home runs in his fabulous career. In fact only Ruth and Mays have hit more. I have been privileged to witness or hear on radio at least 90 per cent of them. He has hit them with more consistency and more power than any other man in the history of the game. In my opinion he is the greatest long ball hitter I ever saw. His power is legendary from both sides of the plate. Here are just a sampling of a few home runs I vividly remember.

It was the early part of Mick's career and the pitcher was a crafty left hander named Chuck Stobbs. The game was in the old Washington park where left field was a long way off. But Mantle took his hard clean perfect swing and the ball started and didn't stop until it was measured 565 feet from home plate. It hit the top of a scoreboard or it might still be going. It was probably the hardest ball ever hit.

There are so many more that Mick hit, the one after the thunderstorm in the early summer of '54. Alex Kellner, a classy left hander, was pitching and it was a fast ball and the ball went out straight. It went to the center field wall and cleared the 461 foot sign in Yankee Stadium. It carried over the monuments and over the high black canvas that they have in center at the stadium and was again measured over 500 feet.

Then there was the one he hit off Pedro Ramos. Batting lefty against the Minnesota right hander Mickey took his best swing and the ball carried to right, high and far over the 344 foot mark at The Stadium. The ball hit the top of the façade covering the third upper deck. No ball has ever been hit out of Yankee Stadium (and this is "the park that Ruth built"), but that ball was the closest; it missed by less than a yard. Not even "The Babe" had ever done that.

Mick has hit at least another dozen that I remember vividly as traveling over five hundred feet. There was the one batting lefty off the curveballing Ray Herbert; Mick's legs were already bad and he couldn't dig in the way he wanted to. Many times that season he would wince in pain as his legs buckled when he took his rip. But this day he somehow mustered up that perfect coordination and power and the ball went again to the centerfield bleachers, again over the monuments, again over 500 feet.

I remember in Shibe Park, Philadelphia, how way back in '53 when he was just twenty-one he hit a ball off Frank Fanovich, a fast left hander. The ball cleared the roof of the upper deck in left and kept going; no one found it to measure. And there was the one he hit off a young left hander named Bob Miller in '54 that went to the opposite field. It went to right center and landed more than half way up in the bleachers. The stadium sign read 407 but the ball cleared it and went at least another hundred feet. It was not hit to his power as he had gone with the pitch and swung easily. I saw it, and I still find it hard to believe.

There are so many more—they were hit in Pittsburgh where Ted Beard hit one and The Bambino did also, all over the roof in right field; and in Detroit where Norm Cash and Ted Williams hit them over the roof. Yes Mick has hit them all over, and either equalled or surpassed all the great long ball feats of every slugger the game has ever produced.

A Special Tribute to the Mick:

Before I close this section on "The Mick" let me tell you younger fans something about this man. His legs are bad now and have been for many years. I can remember being in the dressing room as far back as '52 when I first saw his legs being taped. Rolls, yards were being bandaged on tightly up to his thighs. Supports and bandages and tape; but it was always under the pin stripes and he always went out and played every day. Yes he had guts and he still had speed in those early days. Surprised?

There was a time before all the injuries and all the wounds when he could go to first in 3.1 seconds, faster than Willie Davis, and Sam Jethroe and Ty Cobb. He was a guy who hit a grounder to second, and the fans would roar as he left the plate. Yes it was a thrill just to see him run. I remember those wonderful early years at Joplin and Kansas City, and in his rookie spring training of '51. I remember how he hit and how he ran and how he was going to be the greatest of all the players.

No Mick you are only *one* of the greatest, the torn muscles and cut out cartilages have seen to that. But its enough, damn it, it was more than enough. Thanks for the thrills and the memories Mickey and please play another year.

2. GEORGE HERMAN RUTH: N.Y. YANKEES
1914–1935

It seems strange to rate "The Babe" second, but I'm calling them as I see them, and that is all I can do. Ruth was fabulous, his swing and his power were as perfect as anything in the history of the game. It was short and quick. And the naturalness of that swing made The Babe look like he didn't have to try. It looked so easy.

The Babe hit some measured over 500 feet, and some of the "class old timers" have sworn to me they saw one or two hit over 600 feet. Ruth hit 714 and some of them might have been that long, but they weren't measured—and even if they were they couldn't have gone further than Mickey's. If you want, call it a tie, but if you're younger and have seen Mick, you'll say even the Babe was "number two" for the long ball.

3. JIMMY FOXX: PHILADELPHIA ATHLETICS: 1925–1945

They called him Jimmy "The Beast" and he was strong. He had arms like Killebrew and shoulders and a torso to match. He could hit a ball as far as anybody and he hit 534 home runs in his gigantic career. One of the long balls he hit became a landmark. It was hit in Yankee Stadium and is still talked about and the spot is pointed to with regularity. It was hit to left center off Lefty Gomez and it just missed going out of the park. It was in the direction of the left center field area where the stands, the bullpen and the bleachers divide. The ball missed the bleachers, and missed going out over the pen by twenty little feet. It crashed into the third deck of the left field stands 20 feet too far to the left. It crashed into a chair in the third deck three rows from the very top, breaking its spine. It came that close to going out of the park, and as I have said no ball has ever gone out. If you think it's possible to hit a ball that hard, that far, you have a real imagination. If you're skeptical do what Gomez did—march up to that third deck and go three rows from the top, step off 20 feet and look at home plate. Like "Lefty" you won't remain skeptical—you just won't believe it. That was

Jimmy "The Beast."

4. HARMON KILLEBREW: MINNESOTA TWINS: 1954-

Harmon is enormous. The closer you get to him the more you feel he should have been a strong man in the circus. They say some of his family were just that and I can certainly believe it. He looks like the personification of power when he steps to the plate. He doesn't disappoint anyone either. He has hit more home runs than any player in the past ten years. In 1968 he was hurt but from '59 through '67 he had years of 42, 31, 46, 48, 45, 49, 25, 39, and 44 home runs. Some of them have gone record distances and many have crashed into his own Twin Stadium park. The "white seats" are spots that he reached with these legend makers, and they are all 500 feet away from the plate.

5. FRANK HOWARD: WASHINGTON SENATORS: 1960-

The first time I saw Frank it was in Madison Square Garden. He was on the Ohio State basketball team and a fantastic rebounder. He looked as strong then as Hercules does in those horrible movies, and when I saw him later in the dressing room, he looked even stronger. He is six feet, seven and weighs 285 pounds. And it's all muscle. He is the biggest and strongest man ever to play in the majors, and he can hit a ball as far as anyone. He can't do it with the regularity of a Kiner or a Williams or a Greenberg because he didn't have their God-given talent, but he hits some that will be remembered forever, and one of them was hit in New York in a World Series game off Whitey Ford. It was hit at the shortstop and Kubek leaped, just missing it as the low liner was about 10 feet high. It never elevated to any height but kept going on a line until it crashed into the bleacher wall 457 feet from the plate. A ball has no right to be hit that hard, and The Monster lumbered into third base with a triple, as the players and the fans and Whitey just looked on in dismay. He has hit some in Washington that they marked down also, and big Frank belongs right up there with the legend makers. In fact he might be "Paul Bunyon" if Hollywood ever wants to do the movie.

These are the five men who have been the greatest long ball hitters I can think of. Of course there have been many others—how about young Richie Allen of the Phils, whose brute strength and tremendous swing are starting new legends right now; and how about the "Willies"—Mays, McCovey, Stargell, and Horton. They have hit them with regularity in the past few years. How about some of the others like Gehrig and Greenberg and Ralph Kiner. And before I close don't forget Big Luke Easter of Cleveland in the early '50's and his teammate with that beautiful picture swing—Larry Doby.

Have some more fun; think of the others you have seen or heard about who can hit a baseball with regularity, and then create legends, by hitting them five hundred feet.

5

The Managers

The truest adage in baseball is that "you can't win without the players." The manager can't pitch, hit or field for his ball players. The things that happen on a ball field are always beyond his control. The only possible exception was Lou Boudreau; he did it all and managed, too, in '48. But ultimately without the winning players the manager can only lose.

In the history of the major leagues there have been as many as 30 managerial changes in a single season. If you multiply just one-third of this number by the years the game has been played you'll get an idea of the shuttle service these gutsy generals must ride. They all walk in knowing they'll be fired, and they also know when they win its only a reprieve. Some last a long time, others don't make it two weeks into the season. Many have been forgotten and many were and are never known. Some are buried in the dugout before the first game has been played, others are abused by the fans mercilessly when they go on the field.

But for some it's the only life. Some have been rewarded with immortality. They have become part of the fabric, part of the heart, part of the lore and the spirit of the game.

The six that are spoken of here have won 46 pennants and 24 world championships since 1902. They were more than just successful leaders, though, they were known by every ball player, from "The Babe" to "Mickey" as "The Manager."

1. JOHN J. ("LITTLE NAPOLEON") McGRAW

From 1891 until 1906 he was a major league third baseman, with the Baltimore Orioles and the N.Y. Giants. He was one of the best the game has ever produced with a lifetime average of .334. At the age of twenty-six in 1899 he became a playing-manager for the "old Orioles." In 1900 he did the same for the Cardinals and then went back to Baltimore for two more wonderful years. By the time he came to the Giants as manager and player it was 1903, and three years later he stopped playing and remained as The Manager until 1932.

He won pennants and series championships in those years, and managed Bill Terry, Mel Ott, Frankie Frisch, Christy Mathewson, Carl Hubbell and many, many more. In all he won 10 pennants and 2 world championships in 1905 and again in '21, and in all his years he never managed a quitter. He was a legend and a fighter even then and he was tougher and more baseball man than any of them. What he told you was the law, and what he asked was always done. They hated him and they respected him, and in the end they all loved him. They all called him "The Manager."

2. CORNELIUS (Connie Mack) McGILLICUDDY

He was tall and white haired and always dressed carefully. He wore a suit and a straw hat, not a uniform or cap, but he managed just the same. He was around for a lifetime and many had been children, fathers, and grandfathers by the time he left. He started playing in 1886 and finished his career in 1896 as the catcher for the Pittsburgh team. He never did anything earth shattering but he played, and it was in the National League and that meant a lot. It was still only 1894, and he was a young thirty-two, when he first became a manager. He remained at Pittsburgh through 1896 as player-manager, and soon he would begin a legend. The year was 1901 and he was now living in Philadelphia. He became associated with the Athletics: he was the manager and was to be an owner. He remained in Philadelphia for the next 50 years. Mr. Mack finally left at the age of 88, and the whole baseball world said good bye. He said that "pitching was more than 75 per cent of the game" and he made sure he had the pitchers. He had Eddie Plank and Rube Waddell, and Lefty Grove and Chief Bender and many more. He also had some ball players in those years. There was Jimmy Foxx and "bucketfoot" Al Simmons and a catcher named "Mickey" Cochrane. He won his share of pennants and he won his share of championships, but like the very best of us he will always be remembered for what he was. Connie Mack was "The Manager" for more than fifty years.

3. JOE ("MARSE JOE") McCARTHY

He never played in the majors but how he could general. From 1926 through 1930 he did it for the Chicago Cubs. But it was 1931 that the glory really started. He took over the Yankees and remained through 1946. Later he again took up the calling at Boston and stayed with the Sox until 1950. He was the manager of Keller,

Henrich and Dimaggio; and Rizzuto will always tell you he was the best manager of them all. He won pennants in Chicago in 1929, and then he won many more in New York. In 1932 it was the World Championship in four straight over the Cubs and from 1936 through 1939 it was four more pennants and three Championships. Again he started a streak in '41 and won in '42 and '43. This time he took two championships losing only in '42 when the Cardinals, with the defense of a center fielder named Terry Moore, captured a victory.

In all he was more of a winner than even the statistics or the chronology can tell. In all he was one of the six, one of "The Managers."

4. MILLER ("Hug") HUGGINS

He was a little second baseman for the Cincinnati Reds and later the Cards between 1904 and 1916. At the age of 34 he became a playing-manager for the same St. Louis team. It was 1913 and he remained through 1917. He became a big little man when he moved to the Yankees in 1918. He remained until his death on September 25, 1929. Under the dugout "The Babe" cried.

Miller was the manager of the greatest team in the history of the game. He held Ruth and Gehrig and Combs and all the other monsters in his hand. He was a winner of six pennants and won championships in '23 and of course '27 and again '28. He was quiet and nervous and sort of unhappy. He was Miller and "Hug" and "The Manager" to Ruth and "Lou" and "The Colonel."

5. WILBERT ("Uncle Robby") ROBINSON

He played the game hard for the Baltimore Orioles and the Athletics. He had a lifetime batting average of 286 and he was in the majors as a catcher from 1886 through 1902. It was 1902 when he took over the reins of the old Orioles. At first he only lasted the year. He tried again with Brooklyn in 1914 and this time he found out the manager's secret. He remained a manager until 1931. He was known as 'Uncle Robby" and the players loved him. He suffered through all the hard times. He knew the game and he did his best and he won when he had the tools. In 1916 he won a pennant and in 1920 he did it again.

He had his foot on the dugout steps for many a game and he was called 'The Manager" in every one.

6. CHARLES DILLON ("Casey") STENGEL

To some he was a dentist, to others he was a clown. To some he was an eccentric and to all he will be remembered as "The Manager." He started pulling teeth early in life, and he also played baseball. From 1912 through 1925 he played in Brooklyn, Pittsburgh, Philadelphia, New York, and Boston. Always in the major leagues. He was an outfielder then and his lifetime BA. was a respectable .284.

He managed from 1938 through 1943 for the old Boston Braves. He started a legend, though, in 1949 when he took over the Yankees. He was old in the beginning, with grey in his hair and lines and crevices and ponderous wrinkles all over that beautiful ugly mug. He started with a twinkle and a speech. He also ended with the same twinkle and another speech. He won more World Series games, more pennants and more "big games" than any of them. He broke every record with five consecutive World Championships from that beginning in '49 through '53. He started another streak in '55 with another pennant but Brooklyn and Podres beat him in seven Series games. In '56 he won the championship against the same Brooklyn club. He was still around with his twinkle and his speeches in '57 and '58 and '60. In all he won with the Yankees. In all he was loved by the Mets. In all "Casey" still remains—"The Manager."

6

Bob Kalich Selections of the Greatest Teams in Major League History

I have rated these teams with many thoughts in mind, but the overwhelming one was—which teams would I like to see most, if ever there was a resurrection? Of course it's hard leaving off the Miracle Giants of '51 and the "Koufax" teams, and we can go on and on, but if I had only five chances this is how I would want it.

1. THE GREATEST TEAM IN BASEBALL HISTORY: "MURDERER'S ROW"
The 1927 New York Yankees. Managed from a rocking chair by the always fretting Miller Huggins, they

won 110 games while losing 44. The pennant was clinched early, the final separation was 19 games. In the World Series they did it again, rolling over a powerful Pirate team in four straight games. This great team had the hitting to score in "football" numbers. Some of the individual records of the players still stand.

The Players Who Did Most Were . . .

The Bambino: Ruth hit the immortal "sixty" that year and with a batting average of .356. He also had more than 150 R.B.I.'s.

The Iron Horse: Lou Gehrig followed Ruth in the batting order, he hit 47 home runs and batted .373, and had 175 runs batted in. Ruth scored some of these because he led the league with 158 runs scored.

Long Bob: Bob Meusel played left field and he had one of the greatest arms in the game. Besides he could hit—that year it was .337.

"Colonel": Earl Combs was in center and started it off. He could run, hit and field. His batting average was .356 and he was on base most of the time for Ruth and Gehrig.

"Poosh em up Tony": Tony Lazzeri played second and batted second. He also could hit. .309 for the season.

"Mark": Mark Koenig had class at shortstop and he hit a solid .285 that year.

"Jumpin Joe": Joe Dugan was at third—with his glove.

"Schoolboy": Waite Hoyt won 22 that year. He only lost 8.

"Herb": Herbert Jeffries Pennock was the left handed ace, winning 19 for the '27 club.

"Cy": Wilcey Moore provided the relief. He was in 53 games, saving many and winning 19 while losing only 7. He also started and won the last game of the Series that year.

There were others who contributed, including Pipgras and Bengough, and we salute them all. They were the greatest team in baseball history.

2. THE 1931 PHILADELPHIA ATHLETICS

Managed by the immortal Cornelius McGillicuddy, the team had an easy year. The final standings showed a 13 game differential. They won 107 games during the year and lost only 45. The biggest disappointment came in October when a wild running rookie named John "Pepper" Martin helped the Cardinals upset this fantastic array in seven games.

Some of the great stars of this team were . . .

"Lefty": Bob Grove, who in 1930 won 28 games and lost 5 now really turned it on, and like Koufax 25 years later led the club to a pennant. He won 31 games while losing only 4, and his E.R.A. led the league—2.04 to be exact.

"Mickey": The catcher was Gordon Cochrane and he was the greatest of them all. He hit .349 that year and on October 20, 1931, a baby was born and the father christened it "Mickey" after this great star. The last name was Mantle.

"Bucketfoot": Al Simmons was in the outfield. But when he came to the plate Mr. Mack was much happier. Simmons hit .390 for the year.

"Double X": Jimmy "The beast" Foxx played on the club. He had an off year—for him—hitting only .291. He had injuries through the season. In the series he was healthier, hitting three home runs to provide some value to the three wins. "Double X" was out to prove he could do better the following year and he did. He was healthy and strong and in '32 he hit 58 home runs, and also batted .364.

"Jimmy": Jimmy Dykes took charge of the infield. This gusty little guy could do nothing exceptional, but he knew how to win.

"Moose": George Earnshaw was a classy right hander, winning 21 games and losing only 7.

I would like to see them play again. I would also like to have seen Koufax pitch a year with a Foxx and a Simmons and a Cochrane hitting for him.

3. "THE BRONX BOMBERS": NEW YORK YANKEES, 1941

This team was a great one. Joe ("Marse Joe") McCarthy was the manager. He had it easy. The club won 101 games that year. The pennant was clinched early over the Red Sox. The difference was 17 games. Boston had a guy who hit .406 for the year, but "The Thumper" couldn't take on these Yankees. In the series they beat Brooklyn in five games. It was the year Mickey Owen is remembered for that passed ball—poor Mickey.

The team was great in all positions: depth, defense, and hitting. There was one guy who was the leader; he was a legend even then. "Joltin Joe," The Yankee Clipper, performed miracles the whole year.

"The Yankee Clipper": The Jolter hit .357 for the year, and he led the league in runs batted in with 125. He had doubles, triples, homers, everything. And he did more. The most fabulous record of them all was his that year— the 56 game hitting streak. It went from May 15th through July 16th of 1941. It provided thrills and speculation. It was The Clipper at his best.

"The Scooter" and "The Flash": At shortstop was a young rookie named Phil Rizzuto and he played the position better than anyone. He also hit .307 that year. His partner at second base was Joe Gordon and "The Flash" and "Little Phil" provided the best keystone play of the entire decade—maybe the entire generation.

Gordon had a solid year with the bat also, and in the Series he hit a cool .500.

"Old Reliable" and "King Kong": On Dimaggio's right was Charley Keller and in right field was the then "young reliable" Tommy Henrich. Both of them could hit, and with power and in the clutch. They could field also. It might have been the best Yankee outfield of all time.

"Bill": Bill Dickey was still catching; he was in his twilight days but still caught over 100 games and hit a slick .284.

"Red": The third baseman was Red Rolfe. A .289 lifetime hitter, and an exceptional glove.

"Red" and "Lefty": The club had more pitching in one year than most teams have in two. Red Ruffing won 15 and Gomez had the best winning percentage in the entire league. He was 15 and 5.

"Grandma": When Gomez needed help there was a "fireman" in the bull pen and Johnny Murphy always put it out.

"Spud" and "Tiny": Spurgeon Chandler and Ernie Bonham were also pitching for this great team. Between them they accounted for 19 wins and only lost 10.

Another "Lefty": Marius "Lefty" Russo was also around and he won 14 that year.

There were more pitchers on the team, enough to win an additional 30 games. McCarthy had depth and Connie Mack always said pitching is more than 75 per cent of the game. What would Connie have said if he also had a DiMag and a Keller and a Henrich and a Dickey and a . . . get the point?

4. "THE GAS HOUSE GANG": ST. LOUIS CARDINALS, 1934

It was a pennant race that year and that's what made this gang so great. It finally won by two games with a season record of 98–58. The manager played second base and he hustled for every win.

The Key Players Were . . .

"Fordham Flash": The old man was 36 and he also managed. But he still could show the younger players how to play second and how to hit and how to hustle. He batted .305 for the year.

"Dizzy": Jay Hanna Dean said he would pitch the Cardinals to the pennant, and he did. He won 30 games, losing only 7. In the stretch he pitched his heart out and won all the big ones with very little rest.

"Daffy": "Diz's" younger brother Paul was a rookie that year and besides two important Series wins he had 19 for the year.

"Ducky": Joe Medwick could hit with the best of them and during the year he hit .353 playing in 154 games. In the six categoricals he finished very high on the all time lists.

"Rip": The first baseman was Collins and he tied Mel Ott for the league lead in home runs with 35. Besides that his batting average was .333.

"Pepper": John Martin provided guts and courage. He hit a bloody .289 and did all the things that make a team win. If you never saw him slide head first and in a cloud of dust, you can't say you ever saw real baseball.

This club did more than win games. Like all great teams it captured the imagination of the public and provided a distinct image. This team had flamboyance, color, eccentricity and character. It was bizarre and with some of the greatest personalities the game has ever seen. In the Series against the Tigers they swept in four games with Dizzy and Daffy Dean each winning two games. It was a fabulous team with more than wins and success. It was a "Gashouse Gang" and the people who were there will never forget.

5. "M. and M.": THE 1961 NEW YORK YANKEES

The manager was Ralph "Major" Houk. All he had to do was smoke cigars and stand on front of the dugout steps, the players did the rest. They won 109 games and lost only 53. It was a team that had the most power since the 1927 team—maybe more. Besides they had an infield that played great defense and a pitcher named Ford. In the series they whipped the Reds in five.

Some of the great stars and their achievements

"Mickey" and "Rajah": Mantle hit .317 for the year with 54 home runs. And he provided such fear to the opposition that Maris, batting before him, didn't receive a single intentional walk. It seems impossible but . . . Roger who hit the record 61 and led the league in R.B.I.'s was given none. M. & M. each scored 132 runs to tie for the league leadership. Between them they hit more home runs than any twosome in the game's history for the year—115. Wow . . .

"Ellie" and "Yogi": Howard was the catcher with a .348 batting average. Berra played some outfield and some behind the plate. He was still hitting those clutch home runs, and winning his share of games with his bat.

"Moose": Bill Skowron played solid defensively and offensively. He hit more than 20 home runs during the year.

"Bobby" and "Tony": Richardson and Kubek gave the team the best keystone twins since Rizzuto and Gordon.

"Clete": Boyer played third with a glove that made impossible plays. He looked like "Pie" and Brooks for the whole year.

"Whitey": The great left hander Ford won a total of 25 games and only lost 4. In the series he threw record shutout innings that would continue in other years.

"Luis": Arroyo, the chunky little relief ace, had a

screwball that did tricks and in all he won 15 games losing only five. He also came in time after time to save games.

"Ralph": Terry won 16 games that year and lost only 3. This classy right hander had another of those quiet but good years.

"Bill": Another starter who assisted was Stafford. He won 14 games for the team, and gave them that extra bit of pitching that spells a great staff.

I can still see this team with Mickey and Roger and Whitey. Can you?

6. "THE BROOKLYN BUMS": BROOKLYN DODGERS, 1955

The 1955 Brooklyn Dodgers were beloved by all of Brooklyn. Walter "Smoky" Alston was managing, and he still is. They were the team that finally made the statement "wait till next year" outdated in Brooklyn.

This club beat the Yankees in seven games for the World championship. It was a great series and when it was over there was bedlam in Brooklyn. The Series was the personal and wonderful achievement of a 23 year old left hander named Johnny Podres who won two of the four games, including the seventh. There was also the heroics of a little known left fielder named Sandy Amoros who made an impossible catch and throw, giving the club an all important series win. The team had all those "bums" and they were all great . . .

"The Duke": Snider was the centerfielder, and he was a great one. That year he hit .309 with over 40 home runs and 136 R.B.I.'s. He also led the league in runs scored with 126. Many of the home runs went into Beford Avenue.

"Campy": Roy Campanella did the catching and was most valuable. He hit .318 and with runs batted in and long home runs in plentiful shares.

"Gilly": Gil Hodges played first. His defense was

perfect. Offensively he provided those "automatic" 100 R.B.I.'s and around forty home runs.

"Jackie": Robinson was 35 years old but he still contributed in his inimitable fashion.

"Rocky": Carl Furillo played right field like he owned the property. His arm was like a rifle. He also could hit, .314 that year.

"Pee Wee": Reese was at shortstop with his solid glove and his clutch hitting, class, ability and intelligence.

"Billy": Cox was on third. His hawkish defense was as good as any player who ever played the game.

"Newk": The big right hander won 20 games that year while losing only 5. He was warming up for '56 when Ebbets Field and the bums would really see something, as he would win 27 and lose only 7. Newcombe was a great one.

"Clem": Labine was the reliever. He appeared in 60 games, and stopped most of them from being losses. Besides the saves he won 13.

"Ersk": "Hey Ersk" they cried in Brooklyn and Carl Erskine was there. Slightly built and handsome and with a live fast ball and great curve. He was a "Hoosier" and is, but he always was "Ersk" because of his Brooklyn heart.

They were great—so great they beat the system. Never again would they say in Brooklyn, "Wait till next year."

7

The Courage of a Ball Player

How do you rate the intangibles? The will, the guts, the determination of a ball player. How do you tell the clutch hitter and the steel nerved pitcher from the others? How do you become a money player? That particular entity that can go out and win games in World Series tension, and the stress and strain of the September pennant fight?

I still haven't come up with any final answers but it has to do with something called courage, and these are the players I think showed it best.

1. SANDY KOUFAX (1955–1965): L. A. DODGERS

Did he ever get more than a one run lead? Did he ever do anything wrong? Sandy was there all the time and won everything possible. The Dodgers without him would have been where they are today. With him they won a World championship. And don't forget the arthritis, the pain and the needles . . .

2. TYRUS RAYMOND COBB (1905–1928): DETROIT TIGERS

He played for a quarter of a century. What he did became a legend, what he couldn't do still hasn't been discovered. He would beat you in every way, and would get hit on the elbow if it meant winning a ball game.

3. TOMMY HENRICH (1937–1950): N.Y. YANKEES

They called him "Old Reliable," and who can ever forget the home runs off "Newk" or the others that meant pennants, series games, and money. He could hit in the clutch and he always did.

4. JACKIE ROBINSON (1947–1956): BROOKLYN DODGERS

What could you do to keep him off the bases? He could hit the tar out of the ball and when on base he upset your pitcher to the point where he would balk, throw a home run ball, or just lose the game. He beat you with his glove, his bat, his legs, and his heart. His heart also had other things to prove, and some day he will win all his fights. Jackie was as much a ball player as he is a person. What more could any man be.

5. Lou Boudreau (1938–1952): CLEVELAND INDIANS

The year was 1948 and he managed the team. He also played shortstop, and he had a year. He did everything a manager could want. He hit .355 and in the American

League's only playoff game to date he did better than any manager ever did before or will do again. He played that game against Boston, and he went four for four, with two home runs. Boudreau was the name for "Clutch" that year, and he was also named guts.

6. LOU GEHRIG (1923–1939): N.Y. YANKEES

If ever a player meant class, courage and money in the bank it was the "iron man." His feats are immortal and his ability and leadership made a tradition worth following.

7. MICKEY MANTLE (1951–......): N.Y. YANKEES

How can anyone think of courage without naming him? His inspiration alone makes all his teammates better ball players, better men. His feats are like the Hall of Fame—they personify perfection.

8. JAY HANNA "DIZZY" DEAN (1930–1947): ST. LOUIS CARDINALS

It was a combination of courage, foolishness, and ability that made Diz what he was. He told you he was the greatest, he told you that he would beat you, and in 1934 he did just that.

9. ED "WHITEY" FORD (1950–1967): N.Y. YANKEES

He came up to the parent club in 1950 and he stayed through '67. He won his first nine games in 1950 and he pitched winning baseball every year. And when it came to the big games, and the Series, there never was anyone better. Whitey Ford won ball games—and in the clutch this man of iron will and cool and poise didn't lose. He couldn't lose, and as Casey would tell you, "look it up."

10. GROVER CLEVELAND ALEXANDER (1911–1930): PHILADELPHIA PHILS

He won in the beginning and he won at the end. Remember 1926? He was 39 years old but he beat the Yankees in the Series. He was pitching for the Cardinals then and he had already won the second and sixth games of the series. But now it was the seventh. He came out of the bullpen in the seventh inning, tired and weary and determined. The will was still there. Drawn but determined he struck out Lazerri with the bases loaded, and the seventh game was won by the Cardinals. The score was 3–2 in favor of the "Alexander" Cardinals.

There are many others who had it in their hearts and in their blood as well as the arms and legs and the torsos. I can't mention all of them but I can ask you to remember. How about Monty Stratton and of course Roy Campanella and Clark Griffith and Pete Reiser and Frankie Frisch and Country Slaughter and Eddie Stanky and Lou Brissie and Bobby Shantz and Pepper Martin. It's your turn, and I know you can keep going . . .